BECKY'S
BRUNCH &
BREAKFAST
BOOK

RECIPES AND MENUS TO GET
YOUR DAY OFF TO ITS VERY
BEST START!

REBECCA WALKER

Rebecca Walker has tested each recipe in her home kitchen and has no reason to doubt that recipe ingredients, instructions and directions will work successfully. However, the ingredients, instructions and directions have not necessarily been systematically tested under controlled or standardized conditions, and the cook should not hesitate to test and question procedures and directions before preparation. The recipes in this book have been collected from various sources, and neither Rebecca Walker, nor any contributor, publisher, printer, distributor or seller of this book is responsible for errors or omissions.

1st printing—November 1983
2nd printing—July 1985

Library of Congress Catalog Card Number 83-90856
International Standard Book Number 0-9612284-0-7

Printed in the United States of America
Wimmer Brothers Books
P.O. Box 18408
Memphis, Tennessee 38181-0408
"Cookbooks of Distinction"™

TABLE OF CONTENTS

DEDICATION

This cookbook is dedicated to the many family members and friends who gave generously of their time and culinary skills. Without their enthusiastic support and interest, this project would never have been accomplished.

SPECIAL CONTRIBUTORS INCLUDE:

Azile Albritton

Vicki Barnett

Beverly Blumenthal

Lou Ann Carboy

Janice Green

Barbara Hagood

Shay James

Stephanie Jenkins

Joyce Joiner

Karen LaFleur

Cynthia King

Alisa Long

Janell Long

Robin McIlvaine

Rosemary Shaunfield

Barbara Smith

Catherine Tingle

Judy Walker

Jeannie Weigl

WELCOME TO A BOUNTIFUL BEVY OF BREAKFAST AND BRUNCH!

For most people, the only decision to make at breakfast is whether to grab a donut and cup of coffee—or skip it altogether! The big question is: Can I really face an egg this early in the morning? The only choices are whether to have bacon, sausage or ham; scrambled or fried eggs? Breakfast is the most maligned of our three traditional meals. It seems ideally suited for skipping altogether, getting through as quickly as possible or enduring despite boring routine.

For whatever reasons, surveys show that about half of American adults skip or skimp on breakfast and that only one in five children goes to school with an adequate start for the day.

Everyone knows the guideline of eating breakfast like a king, lunch like a prince and dinner like a pauper—and the fact that most people do just the opposite! Eating breakfast like a king can increase your mental alertness and physical stamina—and give you all day to benefit from and burn up the calories.

This cookbook is dedicated to getting your day off to its very best start! Breakfast can be the most interesting meal of the day, full of endless variety. This book is packed with these possibilities. Oh, you'll find a few of your old favorites, but the idea is to get you away from the routine and predictable.

Experiment with new possibilities. Put the unexpected together for a change. And if you haven't given a brunch, try it as an ideal way to entertain. Brunch fits the schedule of many special occasions, is an economical way to entertain even a crowd and is a more relaxed way to accommodate diverse groups of people. Brunch can be as elegant or casual as you desire. Menus throughout the book will get you started—but let your imagination and ingenuity lead the way!

So whether your goal is a quick "jump start" for the day, a leisurely gourmet feast, the boost to keep you on your diet or an economical way to entertain a crowd—breakfast or brunch is the way. And **BECKY'S BRUNCH & BREAKFAST BOOK** is the means!

WHEN USING THIS COOKBOOK...

Recipes which state:

- "greased pan" means one coated with butter, cooking oil or a food-release spray. If coating with butter is preferred or the pan must also be floured, it is specified. "Greased pan" in Diet and Health sections means one treated with a food-release spray. If a non-stick pan is called for, you may substitute one treated with a food-release spray.

- a packaged item is to be "cooked" means to cook according to package directions unless otherwise specified.

- "heated" or "hot" griddle means one heated until a drop of cold water "dances" on the griddle before rolling off.

- "butter or margarine" in the list of ingredients means either is acceptable. In such cases, "butter" is then used in recipe directions simply to avoid repetition. However, you may use either. When one of the ingredients is preferred, it is called for alone in the list of ingredients.

In measuring ingredients:

- flour is always unsifted unless specified otherwise.

- brown sugar is always "firmly packed".

- "cups" and "ounces" are both given for most cheese amounts for additional ease. Some slight variation between the two measurements may occur due to individual difference in cheese. In most cases, this is of no consequence to the outcome of the recipe.

- "sugar substitute" means either liquid or granulated artificial sweetener. The measurements given apply when the ingredient has equal "sweetness" of sugar. When the product manufacturer states otherwise, adjust measurement accordingly.

Always:

- bake uncovered unless directed otherwise.

WHEN
YOU HAVE LOTS
OF TIME

BRUNCH FOR JUST THE TWO OF YOU

Entrée
Sherried Baked Wonders
Ham Patties

Vegetable
Sesame Hash Browns

Fruit
Frozen Ambrosia Delight

Bread
Orange Coconut Buns

Beverage

Kir   Coffee

Juice

When you have lots of time—may only come on the weekend, vacations, or holidays. But whenever, these recipes are worth the effort.

SPINACH SOUFFLÉ QUICHE

1 (12-ounce) package frozen spinach soufflé, thawed
2 eggs, beaten
3 tablespoons milk
2 teaspoons chopped onions
1 (4-ounce) can mushrooms, drained and coarsely chopped

¾ cup cooked and crumbled hot Italian-style sausage
¾ cup shredded Swiss cheese
1 (9-inch) pastry shell, unbaked

Preheat oven to 400 degrees. Combine all ingredients. Pour into pastry shell. Bake 25 to 30 minutes until lightly browned and knife inserted off center comes out clean. Let stand about 10 minutes before cutting. Serve warm. Serves 4 to 6.

MONTEREY QUICHE

¾ pound hot Italian-style sausage
3 eggs, beaten
1¾ cups hot milk
2 cups (8 ounces) shredded Monterey Jack cheese

1 (4-ounce) can diced green chilies
1 (9-inch) pastry shell, unbaked

Preheat oven to 400 degrees. Crumble sausage, removing casing if necessary. Fry until browned, breaking into small pieces. Drain well. Combine eggs, milk, sausage, cheese and chilies. Turn into pastry shell. Bake 25 to 30 minutes or until knife inserted off center comes out clean. Let stand about 10 minutes before cutting. Serve warm. Serves 6.

CHEESY ONION QUICHE

1 (9-inch) pastry shell, unbaked
2 cups cottage cheese
1/2 cup (2 ounces) shredded
  Swiss cheese
2 eggs, beaten
2 tablespoons chopped chives or
  green onion tops

Salt and freshly ground pepper
  to taste
1/2 (3-ounce) can french-fried
  onion rings, crushed

Preheat oven to 400 degrees. Position rack in lower third of oven. Partially bake pastry shell until golden, 12 to 15 minutes. Remove from oven and reduce temperature to 350 degrees. Combine cottage and Swiss cheeses, eggs, chives or onion tops, salt and pepper. Beat well. Turn into pastry shell; bake 30 minutes. Remove from oven; sprinkle with onion rings. Bake an additional 10 to 15 minutes. Let stand 5 minutes before slicing into wedges. Serves 6 to 8.

ROBIN'S BLINTZ CASSEROLE

3/4 pound ricotta cheese
3/4 pound cottage cheese
2 tablespoons butter or
  margarine, softened

1 teaspoon salt
1 egg, beaten
2 tablespoons sour cream
3 tablespoons sugar

Preheat oven to 350 degrees. Combine all ingredients until smooth. Pour half of crust (see recipe below) into well-greased 9-inch square baking dish. Top with mixture; spread evenly. Cover as evenly as possible with remaining crust. Bake 1 hour or until brown. Serve with hot spiced peaches, fresh fruit or preserves. Serves 6.

Crust:
1/2 cup butter or margarine,
  softened
2 tablespoons sugar
2 eggs, beaten

3/4 cup milk
1 1/2 cups flour
1 teaspoon baking powder

Combine all ingredients thoroughly.

OMELETTES are a real challenge to even the best cooks. Although many techniques are used in preparing omelettes, there are three primary methods. With a little practice, all can be added to your repertoire.

Omelettes offer the opportunity for endless variety. Be creative in adding about 1 tablespoon of filling for each egg.

Some ideas to get you started:
- Swiss cheese and green onions
- Cheddar cheese and crisp bacon bits
- Your favorite recipe of ratatouille
- Avocado slices and bean sprouts
- Sautéed broccoli flowerettes and Cheddar or mozzarella cheese
- Spinach, feta cheese and chopped black olives

Or top a plain omelette with your favorite recipe for Spanish, cheese or mushroom sauce.

 HINT: For all omelettes, begin with your eggs at room temperature. And use non-stick pans or treat them with a food-release spray for even easier handling.

11

The Classic French Omelette is prepared quickly; so be ready to serve. The size of the omelette pan must be in proportion to the number of eggs used. For 2 or 3 eggs, use a 6- or 7-inch pan. When making more servings, prepare individual omelettes or use a pan large enough to accommodate the eggs no deeper than ¼ inch.

CLASSIC FRENCH OMELETTE

2 or 3 eggs	**Dash pepper**
¼ teaspoon salt	**1½ teaspoons butter**

Beat eggs, salt and pepper with a fork until whites and yolks are just blended. Do not overbeat. Melt butter in 6- or 7-inch skillet over high heat. Turn skillet so melting butter coats bottom and sides of pan. When foam subsides and butter is about to lose color, add beaten eggs all at once. Stir rapidly with flat of fork and, at the same time, shake pan back and forth over heat. Stir just until egg mass begins to set. (If adding a filling, spread across center at this point.) Shake pan; omelette should move freely. When omelette is set but not firm, tilt skillet and lift side of omelette nearest the handle with fork. Fold ⅓ of omelette over the center. Run fork around the far side of skillet to make sure omelette is loose and ready to be rolled. Still holding the skillet tilted, give a few sharp blows on base of handle with side of hand to make the far side of omelette fold over onto itself. Let skillet stand over heat 1 or 2 seconds to brown omelette lightly. Hold a warm plate in one hand and grasp skillet handle with the other, palm up. Tilt pan over plate and let omelette roll onto it. Serves 1.

The Firm Omelette requires a little less precise timing.

FIRM OMELETTE

4 eggs, beaten
1/4 cup milk or cream
1/2 teaspoon salt

1/8 teaspoon paprika
1 1/2 tablespoons butter

Combine eggs, milk or cream, salt and paprika. Beat well. Melt butter in a skillet. When moderately hot, add egg mixture. Reduce heat to low and cook. As the edges begin to thicken, lift with a spatula and tilt the skillet to permit the uncooked portion to run to the bottom. Or stick the soft areas with a fork to permit heat to penetrate the bottom crust. When omelette is an even consistency, add any desired fillings and fold over. Serves 2.

The Puffy Oven Omelette requires more preparation time, but is the simplest of all three methods.

PUFFY OVEN OMELETTE

4 eggs, separated
1/4 cup milk or cream
Dash of salt and pepper

2 tablespoons butter or
margarine

Preheat oven to 350 degrees. Beat egg whites until stiff. Beat egg yolks until thick and lemon-colored. Add milk or cream, salt and pepper to egg yolks; blend thoroughly. Fold egg yolk mixture into the beaten whites. Heat butter in medium oven-proof skillet until very hot. Pour in egg mixture and turn temperature to low. Cook slowly until browned underneath, about 10 minutes. Place in oven. Bake 10 to 15 minutes or until light brown on top and no imprint remains when touched lightly with finger. To fold, make a 1/2-inch deep crease across omelette, half-way between handle and other side. Slip a turner under the omelette; tip the skillet to loosen it and fold in half. Roll onto heated platter. Serves 2 to 3.

For perfect **SCRAMBLED EGGS,** heat butter or other fat in moderately hot skillet. Blend together eggs and milk or cream in the amount of 1 tablespoon liquid for each egg. Season to taste. Pour egg mixture into heated skillet and reduce heat to low. As mixture starts to set at bottom and sides, lift the cooked portions with a spatula and turn over gently to cook evenly. You may also lift the thickened portions from the bottom and sides to allow the uncooked mixture to flow underneath and speed cooking. This assures well-formed eggs. When you're in a hurry, simply pull a spoon across the skillet when the eggs are set on the bottom, creating more of a "scramble". In any case, the eggs are ready when almost cooked through but still moist and shiny.

Some good additions—either alone or in combination—to scrambled eggs;
- Sautéed green onions
- Minced fresh herbs
- Shredded cheese
- Sautéed fresh mushrooms
- Deviled ham
- Crisp bacon bits
- Cooked sausage

COUNTRY COTTAGE SCRAMBLE

6 eggs, lightly beaten
⅓ cup milk
½ teaspoon salt
Dash pepper
2 tablespoons butter or margarine

1 (8-ounce) carton cream-style cottage cheese, at room temperature
1 or 2 tablespoons chopped chives or green onion tops

Combine eggs, milk, salt and pepper. In a 10-inch skillet, scramble egg mixture in butter. When eggs are just cooked but still shiny on top, add the cheese and chives or onion tops. Cook quickly, stirring until eggs are cooked as desired and all ingredients are heated through. Serve immediately. Serves 3 to 4.

DANISH DELIGHT

9 eggs at room temperature
1/2 teaspoon tarragon
1/2 teaspoon cracked pepper
1/2 teaspoon salt
1/2 cup white wine or sherry

1/2 teaspoon curry powder
5 1/2 ounces Camembert cheese, cubed
2 tablespoons butter or margarine

Lightly beat the eggs; combine with tarragon, pepper, salt, wine or sherry and curry powder. Blend well. Stir in cheese. In a large skillet, scramble egg mixture in melted butter. Serve immediately. Serves 6 to 8.

CREAMY SCRAMBLED EGGS

8 eggs, lightly beaten
1/3 cup cream
1/2 teaspoon salt
1/8 teaspoon white pepper
1 (3-ounce) package cream cheese, cut into small chunks

1/2 cup ripe olives, sliced or chopped
1 tablespoon butter or margarine

Combine eggs, cream, salt and pepper. Add cream cheese and olives. Melt butter in the top of double boiler over simmering water. Add egg mixture. Cook slowly until set, stirring occasionally. Serves 4 to 6.

EGGS MILANO

1/2 onion, chopped
1 tablespoon butter or margarine
1 tomato, peeled and chopped
1/4 teaspoon marjoram

1/4 teaspoon oregano
4 eggs, beaten
Salt and pepper to taste
Parmesan cheese

In a small skillet, sauté onion in butter until transparent but not brown, about 10 minutes. Add tomato, marjoram and oregano; simmer about 5 minutes or until tomato is tender. Combine eggs, salt and pepper; pour over vegetables. Stir carefully until set. Remove to serving platter and sprinkle with Parmesan cheese. Serves 2.

HINT: Try serving this with Italian sausage links or patties.

15

Almost everything needed for a well-balanced breakfast is included in these next one-dish entrées. Just add fruit and bread and "Breakfast is served!"

CORNED BEEF QUICHE

1 (15½-ounce) can corned beef
  hash
¼ cup finely chopped onion
1 (9-inch) deep dish pastry shell,
  thawed

2 eggs, beaten until frothy
1 (4-ounce) container whipped
  cream cheese with chives
1 cup cottage cheese
¼ teaspoon pepper

Preheat oven to 350 degrees. Combine corned beef hash and onion. Line bottom of pastry shell with the mixture. Combine eggs, cream cheese, cottage cheese and pepper; blend well. Pour over corned beef hash. Bake 50 minutes. Serve warm. Serves 6 to 8.

CORNED BEEF HASH BAKE

2 (15½-ounce) cans corned beef
  hash, warmed
½ to 1 tablespoon butter or
  margarine

6 to 12 eggs
Salt and pepper to taste
3 to 6 tablespoons cream

Preheat oven to 400 degrees. Spread corned beef hash in well-greased individual baking dishes. With back of spoon, make 1 or 2 deep hollows in hash. Dot each hollow with approximately ¼ teaspoon butter. Break an egg into each hollow (1 or 2 for each serving). Season with salt and pepper. Cover each egg with ½ tablespoon cream. Bake 15 to 20 minutes or until eggs are set as desired. Serves 6.

NOTE: When increasing this recipe to serve a crowd, spread desired amount of corned beef hash in glass baking dish that is large enough to accommodate it at about ¾-inch depth. Make as many hollows as needed for 1 or 2 eggs per person. Dot hollows with butter or margarine and pour ½ tablespoon cream over each egg. Bake as directed. Divide into squares and serve.

FARMER'S FAVORITE BREAKFAST

6 slices bacon, diced
1 small green pepper, diced
2 tablespoons diced onions
2 cooked potatoes, peeled and
    diced
Salt and pepper to taste
1/2 cup (2 ounces) shredded
    Cheddar cheese
6 eggs, lightly beaten

In a large skillet, fry bacon until crisp. Remove with a slotted spoon and drain on paper towels. Drain off all but 3 tablespoons bacon drippings. Place the green pepper, onion and potatoes in the skillet; sprinkle with salt and pepper. Cook, stirring over medium heat, until potatoes are golden. Sprinkle cheese over the mixture and stir until melted. Combine eggs, salt and pepper. Return bacon to skillet; pour eggs over all. Scramble over low heat until set. Serves 4.

ITALIAN SAUSAGE SCRAMBLE

1/2 pound Italian sweet sausage
2 tablespoons cooking oil
1 cup peeled and diced cooked
    potatoes
1/2 medium onion, chopped
1/4 green pepper, chopped
1 cup peeled, seeded and
    chopped tomatoes
8 eggs, beaten
1/4 cup heavy cream
Salt and pepper to taste
Italian bread, sliced thick,
    buttered and toasted
Oregano
Parmesan cheese

Crumble sausage, removing casing if necessary. In a large skillet, fry sausage in oil until no longer pink. Add potatoes, onion and green pepper. Sauté, stirring occasionally, until potatoes are brown and onions and pepper are soft. Add tomatoes and cook 1 minute. Combine eggs, cream, salt and pepper; stir into sausage mixture. Scramble over medium heat until eggs are set. Spoon mixture over the toast and sprinkle with oregano and cheese. Serves 6.

VARIATION: All amounts may be divided in half. Prepare the sausage and vegetable mixture as directed. Remove from skillet with a slotted spoon and keep warm. Pour the egg mixture into the skillet and prepare as an omelette. When ready to fold, place the sausage and vegetable mixture on one half. Fold over and sprinkle with the oregano and cheese. Serve the toast on the side. Serves 2 to 3.

BEAUTIFUL BUFFET EGGS

1/4 cup finely sliced green onion
  tops
3 tablespoons butter or
  margarine

9 eggs, well beaten
2 (2 1/2-ounce) jars dried beef,
  cut into small strips
1 cup cottage cheese

In a large skillet, sauté onion tops in butter until tender. Combine eggs, dried beef and cottage cheese. Add egg mixture to onion and scramble. Serves 6.

NOTE: Try Beautiful Buffet Eggs served in brioche. Warm brioches in 350 degree oven while scrambling eggs. Slice the tops off the brioches and scoop out the soft center. Fill with the eggs and top with brioche "caps". Delicious.

CORNED BEEF BREAKFAST MUFFINS

1 (12-ounce) can corned beef
2 tablespoons minced green
  onions
5 eggs

1/2 teaspoon salt
1 tablespoon cooking oil
2 English muffins, split and
  toasted

Combine corned beef, green onions, 1 egg and salt. Shape mixture into 4 firm patties. Fry patties about 10 minutes in hot oil over low heat until lightly browned, carefully turning once. With spoon, make an indentation in center of each patty; break an egg into each. Cover and cook 10 to 15 minutes until eggs are cooked as desired. To serve, place a corned beef patty on each muffin half. Serves 2 to 4.

WESTERN SCRAMBLE

12 eggs, beaten
2/3 cup water
1/2 medium green pepper, diced
1 (4-ounce) package sliced ham,
  diced

1 teaspoon grated onion
1/2 teaspoon salt
1/4 teaspoon cracked pepper
4 tablespoons butter or
  margarine

Combine eggs, water, green pepper, ham, onion, salt and pepper. Melt butter in a large skillet over medium heat. Add egg mixture; reduce heat to medium low. Scramble egg mixture until just set. Serves 6.

Eggs and cheese are natural complements. And when you add the zest of chilies and spices in these dishes, you have the Southwestern regional favorites known as "Tex-Mex".

FIESTA CASSEROLE

1 pound bulk sausage, crumbled
¼ pound fresh mushrooms,
    chopped
1 medium onion, diced
Salt and freshly ground pepper
    to taste
6 eggs
3 tablespoons sour cream
6 tablespoons Salsa (bottled
    or see page 102)

2 cups (8 ounces) shredded
    Cheddar cheese
2 cups (8 ounces) shredded
    mozzarella cheese
2 cups (8 ounces) shredded
    pasteurized process cheese
    loaf

Preheat oven to 400 degrees. Sauté sausage, mushrooms and onion in large skillet over medium-high heat until sausage is completely cooked. Season with salt and pepper. Drain well and set aside. Combine eggs and sour cream in blender; whip 1 minute. Turn into greased 9x13-inch baking dish. Bake until eggs are softly set, 4 to 7 minutes. Spoon Salsa evenly over top. Spread sausage mixture overall; top with combined cheeses. Preheat broiler. To serve immediately, broil until cheeses are melted. Serves 6.

TO PREPARE IN ADVANCE: When assembled, cover and refrigerate until serving time. Preheat oven to 325 degrees. Bake until cheeses are melted, about 30 minutes.

ROSIE'S EGGS MEXICANA

5 eggs, beaten
2 tablespoons butter or
   margarine, melted
1/4 cup flour
1/2 teaspoon baking powder
1 (8-ounce) carton cream-
   style cottage cheese

2 cups (8 ounces) shredded
   Monterey Jack cheese
1 (4-ounce) can chopped
   green chilies, drained

Preheat oven to 400 degrees. Combine eggs, butter, flour and baking powder; mix well. Stir in the cheeses and chilies. Pour into well-greased 8-inch square baking dish. Bake 10 minutes; reduce temperature to 350 degrees and bake another 20 minutes or until set. Serves 6.

BREAKFAST ENCHILADAS

5 eggs, beaten
2 tablespoons milk
1/4 cup diced green chilies
Salt and pepper to taste

2 tablespoons butter or
   margarine
4 corn tortillas
3/4 cup shredded Cheddar cheese

Preheat broiler. Combine eggs, milk, chilies, salt and pepper. In a skillet over medium-low heat, scramble egg mixture in melted butter. Cook until firm as desired. Dip tortillas 1 at a time into hot Enchilada Sauce (see recipe below) until soft. Spoon 1/4 of the eggs down center of each tortilla. Roll up and place, seam side down, in a single layer in a greased 10x6-inch glass baking dish. Bring remaining Sauce to boil. Pour evenly over rolled tortillas; sprinkle with cheese. Broil about 4 inches from heat 2 to 3 minutes or until cheese melts. Serves 2.

Enchilada Sauce:
1 small onion, chopped
1/2 cup chopped green pepper
1 1/2 tablespoons cooking oil

1 (15-ounce) can tomato sauce
1 1/2 teaspoons chili powder

In a small skillet over medium heat, sauté onion and green pepper in oil until onion is limp. Stir in tomato sauce and chili powder. Reduce heat to low and simmer while the eggs are cooking.

MUFFINS OLÉ

½ cup Gayle's Glorious
    Guacamole (see page 102)
2 English muffins, split and
    warmed
6 slices bacon, fried crisp
    and crumbled

4 eggs
1 tablespoon water
1 tablespoon butter or
    margarine
4 thin slices Cheddar or
    Monterey Jack cheese

Preheat broiler. Spread equal amount of Guacamole (or use avocado slices) on each muffin half. Sprinkle bacon over all. Beat the eggs and water together. Melt butter in a medium skillet and scramble the eggs. Spoon equal amounts of eggs over each muffin half. Top each with a slice of cheese. Place under broiler until cheese melts. Serves 2 to 4.

KING'S MAGNIFICO EGGS

2 (4-ounce) cans whole green
    chilies
4 cups (16 ounces) shredded
    Cheddar cheese

6 eggs
1½ cups biscuit mix
4 cups milk
Salt and pepper to taste

Preheat oven to 350 degrees. Split and seed chilies. Spread on bottom of well-greased 9x13-inch baking dish. Cover with cheese. Beat eggs, biscuit mix, milk, salt and pepper with rotary beater until smooth. Pour over cheese. Bake 1 hour or until firm in center. Let stand 10 minutes before cutting. Serves 8.

JOE'S FAMOUS HUEVOS RANCHEROS

1 medium onion, chopped
2 tablespoons butter or
    margarine
1 (14½-ounce) can whole
    tomatoes
Fresh jalapeño pepper, seeded
    and finely chopped

½ teaspoon salt, or to taste
Corn tortillas
Cooking oil
Eggs

Sauté onion in butter until limp, about 5 minutes. Stir in tomatoes and cook, breaking them up. Add fresh jalapeño peppers (not canned or pickled) according to taste (usually ½ to 1 whole pepper is sufficient). Add salt and simmer uncovered until flavors are well blended and sauce is thickened, about 30 minutes. To serve, dip tortillas one at a time in heated oil until soft, about 2 seconds. Top with fried or scrambled eggs. Spoon hot sauce over all. Serves 4.

DAYBREAK TOSTADOS

6 flour tortillas
8 eggs, scrambled
3 cups (12 ounces) shredded
    Cheddar or Monterey Jack
    cheese
1 pound bacon, fried, drained
    and crumbled

1 medium onion, finely chopped
1 cup Gayle's Glorious
    Guacamole (see page 102)
¼ cup sliced ripe olives
Sour cream
Salsa (bottled or see page 102)

Preheat oven to 350 degrees. Wrap tortillas tightly in foil; warm 15 minutes. Remove from oven; preheat broiler. Layer scrambled eggs and cheese evenly on the tortillas; broil just long enough to melt the cheese. Top with layers of bacon, onion, Guacamole, olives and sour cream. Serve Salsa in a separate bowl; add to taste. Serves 6.

MEXICAN SCRAMBLE

6 corn tortillas
Cooking oil
1 small onion, finely chopped
2 tablespoons butter or
   margarine
6 to 8 tablespoons chopped
   green chilies

12 eggs, beaten
¼ cup milk
Salt and pepper to taste
⅔ cup shredded Monterey Jack
   cheese

Cut the tortillas into triangles. Sauté in hot oil until soft but not crisp, about 2 seconds. In a large skillet, sauté the onion in butter until soft, about 5 minutes. Stir in chilies. Combine eggs, milk, salt and pepper. Stir in cheese and tortillas. Pour into skillet with the onion mixture. Cook, stirring until eggs are set. Serves 6 to 8.

SUNSHINE TOSTADOS

Butter or margarine
4 corn or flour tortillas
2 cups (8 ounces) shredded
   Monterey Jack or Cheddar
   cheese
8 tablespoons chopped green
   chilies
1⅓ cups shredded lettuce

4 tablespoons thinly sliced
   green onion
1 (4-ounce) package cooked ham
4 to 8 eggs, poached
Cherry tomato halves
Salsa (bottled or see page 102)
Sour cream

Preheat oven to 400 degrees. Lightly butter one side of tortillas. Place on a baking sheet; bake until lightly toasted, 3 to 5 minutes. Remove from oven; turn tortillas over and sprinkle evenly with cheese and chilies. Return to oven 3 minutes or until cheese is bubbly. Remove from oven and sprinkle each tortilla evenly with lettuce, onion and ham. Top each Tostado with 1 or 2 eggs. Garnish with tomatoes. Serve Salsa and sour cream in separate bowls to spoon over as desired. Serves 4.

BREAKFAST TACO

Roll your favorite combination of eggs scrambled with sausage, cheese, onions and potatoes in warmed flour tortilla. Serve with Salsa and sour cream—Olé!

This next section will satisfy the most gourmet of palates—and impress even the boss's wife!

BREAKFAST EN CROÛTE

1 (17¼-ounce) package frozen
    puff pastry sheets
1 pound boiled ham slices
8 to 16 eggs

16 ounces Borsin or other
    spiced soft cheese
1 egg
1 teaspoon water

Preheat oven to 425 degrees. Remove pastry sheets from freezer and thaw 20 minutes. Gently unfold and cut each sheet into 4 squares. Cut a ½-inch hole in the center of each. Slice ham into julienne strips; sprinkle half into 8 well-greased individual baking dishes. Top with 1 or 2 eggs. Cut cheese into small cubes; sprinkle over eggs. Cover with remaining ham strips. Place a pastry sheet over the top of each baking dish, pressing edges onto the dish tightly. Beat the egg with water. Brush lightly over pastry. Bake 15 to 20 minutes or until eggs are set and pastry is puffed and golden brown. Serves 8.

TIP: When Breakfast en Croûte is assembled, you can cover and refrigerate for up to 12 hours before baking. And if your baking dishes are large, either use an additional package of pastry sheets or roll out each square to fit.

GOURMET'S DELIGHT

12 canned artichoke bottoms,
    drained
2 (9-ounce) packages frozen
    creamed spinach, cooked

12 eggs, poached
2 cups Hollandaise sauce

Preheat broiler. In a saucepan, warm artichoke bottoms in salted water until heated through. Place 2 artichoke bottoms in each of 6 well-greased individual baking dishes; fill with the spinach. Place one poached egg on each spinach-filled artichoke bottom. Top with your favorite recipe or packaged Hollandaise sauce (or see page 102). Run under broiler for few minutes until sauce is lightly browned. Serve immediately. Serves 6.

To **POACH EGGS:** Use a specially-designed pan according to manufacturer's directions. Or if you're more adventuresome, try this:

> Bring about 2 inches of water to boil in a shallow pan. Add 1 tablespoon vinegar. Reduce heat so water just simmers. Break an egg into a small bowl or saucer and slip it into the water. Add additional eggs the same way, but don't let them touch each other. Cook 3 to 5 minutes or until firm as desired. Remove with a slotted spoon and drain well.

SAUCY EGGS MORNAY

6 thin slices ham
Butter or margarine
3 English muffins, split,
    buttered and toasted

6 eggs, poached
1 tablespoon chopped chives

Lightly brown ham in small amount of butter. Place ham slice on each muffin half and top with poached egg. Keep warm while preparing Mornay Sauce (see recipe below). Pour Mornay Sauce over eggs and sprinkle with chives. Serve immediately. Serves 3 to 6.

Mornay Sauce:
3 tablespoons butter or
    margarine
3 tablespoons flour
3/4 teaspoon salt

1/4 teaspoon nutmeg
Dash pepper
1 cup light cream
1/4 cup dry white wine
1/3 cup shredded Swiss cheese

Melt butter in saucepan. Blend in flour, salt, nutmeg and pepper. Stir until smooth and bubbly. Add cream all at once and cook quickly, stirring constantly until mixture thickens and bubbles. Stir in wine. Add cheese and stir until melted. Use at once.

EGGS BENEDICT

Hollandaise sauce
8 slices Canadian-style bacon or
  ham
Butter or margarine
4 English muffins, split and
  warmed

8 eggs, poached
Paprika
Ripe olives

Preheat oven to 200 degrees. Prepare your favorite recipe or packaged Hollandaise sauce (or see page 102). Keep sauce warm. Sauté bacon or ham in a small amount of butter. Top each muffin half with a bacon or ham slice. Place eggs on top. Just before serving, spoon sauce over eggs and sprinkle with paprika. Garnish with a sliver of ripe olive if desired. Serves 4.

SHERRIED BAKED WONDERS

2 teaspoons chopped green
  onions
4 tablespoons butter
1 cup (4 ounces) shredded
  Swiss cheese
8 eggs

Salt and pepper to taste
Dash basil
1 cup sour cream
¼ cup heavy cream
¼ cup dry sherry

Preheat oven to 325 degrees. In a small skillet, sauté green onions in butter until butter is golden brown. Remove onion with a slotted spoon and discard. Pour about 4 teaspoons of the browned butter into 4 well-greased individual baking dishes. Top with ½ cup cheese. Place 2 eggs in each dish; season with salt, pepper and basil. Combine sour cream, heavy cream and sherry. Pour mixture over the eggs; top with remaining cheese. Drizzle remaining browned butter over all. Place baking dishes in a pan containing 1-inch boiling water. Bake 15 minutes or until eggs are firm. Serves 4.

CLASSIC EGGS FLORENTINE

2 (10-ounce) packages chopped
  spinach, cooked and drained
12 eggs, poached

Grated Swiss or Parmesan
  cheese

Preheat broiler. Layer spinach in bottom of 6 greased individual shallow baking dishes (1-cup size). Place 2 eggs in each of the spinach-lined dishes. Cover with Florentine Sauce (see recipe below); sprinkle each dish with about 1 teaspoon cheese. Broil 6 inches from heat 4 to 5 minutes or until lightly browned. Serves 6.

Florentine Sauce:

2 tablespoons finely chopped
  onion
4 tablespoons butter or
  margarine
¼ cup flour
½ teaspoon salt
⅛ teaspoon pepper

Dash nutmeg
1½ cups milk
½ cup light cream
1 egg yolk
½ cup (2 ounces) grated Swiss
  or Parmesan cheese

In a medium-size heavy saucepan, sauté onion in melted butter until golden, about 5 minutes. Remove from heat. Add flour, salt, pepper and nutmeg. Stir until smooth. Add milk all at once; blend. Add cream, a small amount at a time, stirring after each addition. Return to heat. Bring mixture to boil over medium heat, stirring constantly. Reduce heat and simmer 3 minutes, stirring. In a small bowl, beat egg yolk with a fork. Stir in about ½ cup hot sauce; mix well. Add egg yolk-sauce mixture along with the grated cheese to sauce in the saucepan, stirring to blend well. Cook, stirring over low heat until sauce is thickened and cheese is melted. Do not boil. Keep warm until ready to serve by placing in pan of hot water.

DEVILISH EGG DIVAN

2 (10-ounce) packages frozen
   broccoli spears, cooked
   and drained
6 eggs, hard boiled and cooled
3 tablespoons mayonnaise
2 teaspoons instant minced
   onions

1 teaspoon prepared mustard
1/2 teaspoon Worcestershire
   sauce
1 (4 1/2-ounce) can deviled ham
Paprika

Preheat oven to 350 degrees. Arrange broccoli in one greased 10x6-inch shallow baking dish or 6 individual ramekins. (Ramekins are preferred for a simpler and more attractive presentation.) Slice the eggs in half lengthwise. Remove yolks and mash. Mix with mayonnaise, onion, mustard, Worcestershire sauce and half the deviled ham. Place about half the remaining ham in hollow of egg whites. Fill with yolk mixture (it will cover the entire egg) and top with last of the ham. Arrange eggs on the broccoli; cover with White Sauce (see recipe below). Sprinkle with paprika. Bake 20 minutes. Serves 6.

White Sauce:
2 tablespoons butter or
   margarine
2 tablespoons flour
1/2 teaspoon salt
1 1/4 cups milk

1 cup (4 ounces) diced sharp
   Cheddar cheese
1/2 teaspoon Worcestershire
   sauce

Melt butter in a saucepan. Blend in flour and salt until smooth. Add milk all at once. Cook over medium-high heat, stirring constantly until mixture thickens and bubbles. Remove from heat. Add cheese and Worcestershire sauce. Stir until cheese melts.

PIQUANT BAKED EGGS

4 strips bacon
4 eggs
2 tablespoons grated Parmesan
   cheese

1 tablespoon melted butter or
   margarine
4 dashes red pepper sauce

Preheat oven to 350 degrees. Fry bacon until transparent but not crisp. Drain. Place bacon strips around sides of 2 well-greased individual baking dishes. Carefully break 2 eggs into each dish; sprinkle with cheese. Combine butter and hot sauce; pour half over eggs in each dish. Bake 15 minutes or until eggs are set. Serves 2.

ROLLED SWISS OMELETTE

½ cup mayonnaise
2 tablespoons flour
12 eggs, separated
1 cup milk
½ teaspoon salt

⅛ teaspoon pepper
1½ cups finely chopped ham
1 cup (4 ounces) shredded
    Swiss cheese
¼ cup chopped green onion

Preheat oven to 425 degrees. In a saucepan, combine mayonnaise and flour. Beat egg yolks until smooth. Add yolks and milk to saucepan; cook, stirring constantly over low heat until thickened. Remove from heat; cool 15 minutes. Beat egg whites until stiff peaks form. Fold mayonnaise/yolk mixture, salt and pepper into whites. Pour into 15½x10½-inch jellyroll pan that has been lined with waxed paper and brushed thoroughly with mayonnaise. Bake 20 minutes. Invert pan on towel; carefully remove waxed paper. Combine ham, cheese and onion; spread evenly over omelette. Roll from narrow end, lifting with towel while rolling. Serve seam side down on serving platter. Top with Mustard Sauce (see recipe below). Serves 6 to 8.

Mustard Sauce:
1 cup mayonnaise
2 tablespoons prepared mustard

2 tablespoons chopped green
    onion

Combine all ingredients; mix well.

SUNDAY SCRAMBLE

4 brioches (prepared from recipe
    on page 96 or purchased
    at bakery)
7 eggs
¼ cup milk
½ teaspoon salt
Dash pepper

2 tablespoons butter or
    margarine
1 (3-ounce) package cream
    cheese with chives, cut into
    ½-inch cubes
Chopped parsley or chives

Preheat oven to 350 degrees. Heat brioches on a cookie sheet while preparing eggs. Combine eggs, milk, salt and pepper; beat with rotary beater until just blended. In a large skillet over low heat, scramble the egg mixture in butter. When eggs are set but still moist, add cheese; continue cooking until eggs are set as desired and heated through. Cut off tops of brioches; set aside. Scoop the soft inside from center of the brioche; spoon scrambled eggs into the cavity. Sprinkle with parsley or chives and replace the tops. Serves 4.

MUSHROOM OMELETTE ROLL

1 pound mushrooms, finely
   chopped
4 tablespoons butter or
   margarine
1 (³/₄- to 1-ounce) package white
   sauce mix

1 cup milk
12 eggs, separated
1 cup (4 ounces) shredded
   Swiss cheese

Preheat oven to 400 degrees. In a large skillet over medium-low heat, sauté mushrooms in butter until tender, about 10 minutes. Keep warm. Prepare white sauce mix with 1 cup milk as label directs for a medium white sauce; set aside. In small bowl with fork or wire whisk, beat egg yolks lightly. Stir small amount of hot white sauce into yolks. Slowly pour egg yolk mixture into remaining white sauce; stir rapidly to prevent lumping. Cook mixture over medium heat, stirring until thickened. Cool mixture slightly, about 15 minutes. In large bowl with rotary beater at high speed, beat egg whites until stiff peaks form. Gently fold yolk mixture into egg whites. Spread mixture evenly in 15½x10½-inch jellyroll pan that has been lined with waxed paper and greased thoroughly. Bake 25 minutes or until omelette is puffy and golden brown. Immediately invert omelette onto clean cloth towel. Carefully peel off waxed paper; discard. Sprinkle mushrooms and Swiss cheese evenly over omelette to within ¼ inch of edges. Starting at narrow end, roll up omelette jelly-roll fashion, lifting towel while rolling. Serve seam side down on warm platter. Serves 6.

CRÊPES are great to have on hand—they can turn the most humble scrambled eggs into an elegant meal. To freeze prepared crêpes for ready use, simply store in plastic wrap; there's no need to wrap individually for crêpes will separate easily when thawed. If the recipe requires warmed crêpes, place in a covered baking dish and pop into a warm oven a few minutes.

Here are a couple of recipes for crêpes and several recipes using them. But don't let these be your only guide—experiment with a variety of scrambled eggs and topping combinations for your own special creations.

SIMPLY DELICIOUS CRÊPES

2 eggs, beaten
1 cup milk
1 cup sifted flour

1 tablespoon melted butter or
   margarine
Pinch of salt

Combine eggs and milk, mixing well. Gradually pour in the flour, stirring constantly with a wire whisk or fork until mixture is smooth. Add butter and salt. Mix until smooth. The batter should have the consistency of fresh cream. Crêpes may be cooked on a dome-shaped griddle according to manufacturer's directions. Or heat a small skillet with sloping sides over moderately high heat; brush lightly with butter or oil. Pour a scant ¼ cup batter into middle of pan. Quickly tilt pan in all directions so that batter covers pan with a thin film. Cook approximately 3 minutes; top should be set and the underside golden. Do not turn. Slide crêpes onto plate and separate with waxed paper. Continue until all batter is used. Yields twenty to twenty-four 5-inch crêpes.

SIMPLY HEALTHY CRÊPES

2 eggs, beaten
1 cup milk
1 cup fine-ground whole wheat
   flour

⅓ cup toasted wheat germ
2 tablespoons melted butter
   or margarine
Pinch of salt

Combine eggs and milk, mixing well. Gradually pour flour and wheat germ into the milk and eggs, stirring constantly with a wire whisk or fork until mixture is smooth. Add butter and salt; blend well. Proceed with cooking as directed in Simply Delicious Crêpes. Yields twenty to twenty-four 5-inch crêpes.

SWISS BREAKFAST CRÊPES

8 eggs
⅓ cup milk or cream
Dash each salt and pepper
½ pound diced, cooked ham

1 tablespoon butter or
   margarine
8 crêpes
8 thin slices Swiss cheese

Preheat oven to 350 degrees. Combine eggs with milk or cream; beat well. Add salt, pepper and ham. In a skillet, scramble eggs in melted butter. Spoon eggs onto center of crêpes; roll sides over eggs. Place crêpes seam-side down in greased 9x13-inch baking dish. Top each with a slice of cheese. Bake 10 minutes or until cheese is melted and crêpes are heated through. Yields 8 crêpes.

SUNSHINE SAUSAGE CRÊPES

8 ounces bulk sausage
6 eggs, beaten
1/3 cup milk
1/2 teaspoon salt

Dash pepper
6 crêpes, warmed
Maple syrup

In a skillet, fry sausage until thoroughly cooked. Drain well and set aside. Pour off all but 2 tablespoons sausage fat. Combine eggs, milk, salt and pepper; scramble in reserved fat. Return sausage to skillet and heat through. Spoon scrambled eggs onto center of crêpes; roll sides over eggs. Top with small amount of maple syrup. Yields 6 crêpes.

BEVERLY'S BEST BLINTZES

2 cups sifted flour
4 eggs, well beaten
1 cup milk

1 cup water
4 tablespoons butter or
    margarine, melted

Re-sift flour into eggs; beat until smooth. If too thick to beat easily, add a little of the milk and water. When smooth, add all of the liquids and butter. (If lumpy, place in blender and whirl briefly.) Chill batter 1 hour. When ready to cook, prepare as directed in Simply Delicious Crêpes (see page 31). When all the batter has been prepared, roll about 3 tablespoons Cheese Filling (see recipe below) into a ball; place in center of browned side of crêpe. Fold one side over and then the other. Fold remaining sides so that no filling is visible; flatten. Heat additional butter in skillet; brown blintzes on all sides. If preferred, bake in 375 degree oven 15 to 20 minutes or until golden; turn once. Serve with sour cream, fresh strawberries, strawberry preserves, or a sprinkling of powdered sugar or cinnamon. Yields 25 to 30 blintzes.

Cheese Filling:
2 (8-ounce) packages cream
    cheese, softened
2 (16-ounce) bags dry cottage
    cheese

2 egg yolks
1 teaspoon salt
1 tablespoon melted butter or
    margarine (optional)

Combine cheeses and mash with a fork. Using rotary beater, add remaining ingredients. If filling is too dry, add another egg yolk. Chill.

HINT: Blintzes can be prepared and frozen before browning. When ready to serve, remove from freezer—there's no need to thaw—and brown slowly in butter or margarine.

WHEN YOU'RE IN A HURRY

WELCOME HOME BRUNCH

Entrée
Sausage and Egg Brunch Bake

Vegetable
Down-Home Fried Potatoes

Bread
Mother's Angel Biscuits
Orange-Strawberry Preserves   Apricot Marmalade

Fruit
Honey of a Fruit Salad

Beverage
Coffee   Assorted Juices

When You're in a Hurry—may seem like most of the time! So many homemakers now play the dual role of career woman, leaving little time to prepare a good breakfast. These recipes fit into that busy schedule—giving the whole family a good start for the day!

PITA BREAKFAST SANDWICHES

For a neat and mobile breakfast, nothing is better than Pita Breakfast Sandwiches. Simply wrap Pita Bread in foil and pop into a 375 degree oven for 15 minutes. Then fill with your favorite recipe of scrambled eggs. If desired, the sandwiches may be re-wrapped and returned to a warm oven until ready to serve.

The following is a good scrambled egg recipe to try.

PITA-PERFECT SCRAMBLE

½ pound bacon, diced, fried
    crisp and drained
¼ cup chopped onion
½ cup biscuit mix
4 eggs

1¼ cups milk
¼ teaspoon salt
⅛ teaspoon pepper
½ cup (2 ounces) shredded
    Cheddar or Swiss cheese

Preheat oven to 375 degrees. Spread bacon and onion in bottom of well-greased 1½-quart casserole. Beat biscuit mix, eggs, milk, salt and pepper with rotary beater until almost smooth. Slowly pour egg mixture over bacon and onion; sprinkle with cheese. Bake 35 minutes or until knife inserted in center comes out clean. Serve alone or spoon into warmed Pita Bread. Serves 4 to 6.

HELP FOR A HURRIED MORNING: Place bacon and onion in prepared casserole and egg mixture in a jar. Cover and refrigerate the night before. The next morning, proceed as directed, popping the Pita Bread into the oven the last 15 minutes the eggs are baking.

BEEFY CHEESE RAREBIT

4 tablespoons butter or
   margarine
¼ cup flour
1¾ cups milk
1 cup (4 ounces) shredded
   Cheddar cheese
2 (2½-ounce) jars dried beef,
   chopped

½ teaspoon Worcestershire
   sauce
Dash paprika
4 slices bread, toasted on
   both sides

Melt butter in medium skillet; stir in flour. Slowly add milk, stirring constantly until thickened. Reduce heat to low; stir in cheese. Add dried beef, Worcestershire sauce and paprika. Heat 5 minutes or until cheese is melted and rarebit is bubbly. Serve over toast. Serves 4.

SAUSAGE SCRAMBLEBURGERS

½ pound bulk sausage
2 tablespoons chopped green
   pepper
2 tablespoons finely sliced
   green onion
4 eggs, beaten

4 tablespoons milk or cream
½ teaspoon salt
⅛ teaspoon pepper
2 onion rolls, split, buttered
   and toasted

Form sausage into 2 patties large enough to cover rolls. Fry in medium skillet until thoroughly cooked. Remove from skillet; drain on paper towels and keep warm. Drain all but 1 tablespoon of the sausage fat. Sauté green pepper and onion in reserved fat until tender, about 5 minutes. Combine eggs, milk or cream, salt and pepper; blend thoroughly. Pour egg mixture over vegetables. Scramble gently to keep well formed. Place sausage patties on bottom half of rolls; top with scrambled eggs and remaining roll halves. Serve immediately. Serves 2.

VARIATION: Cook the bulk sausage, breaking into small pieces. Proceed as recipe directs, returning sausage to the skillet when the egg mixture is added to the vegetables.

Here are a couple quick versions of the classic Eggs Florentine.

QUICKIE EGGS FLORENTINE

2 (10-ounce) packages frozen
    chopped spinach, cooked
    and drained
4 to 8 eggs
Salt and pepper to taste

1 (10¾-ounce) can cream of
    mushroom soup
1½ cups (6 ounces) shredded
    Cheddar cheese

Preheat oven to 350 degrees. Grease an 8-inch square baking dish or 4 individual ramekins. Line bottoms with spinach. Make 4 to 8 hollows in spinach with back of a spoon; break an egg into each. Sprinkle with salt and pepper. In a saucepan, heat soup and 1 cup cheese until well blended and cheese is melted. Pour over eggs. Sprinkle remaining cheese on top. Bake 15 to 30 minutes or until eggs are set as desired. Serves 4.

FLORENTINE SANDWICHES

1 (10-ounce) package chopped
    frozen spinach, thawed and
    drained
2 tablespoons butter or
    margarine
Salt and pepper to taste
2 tomatoes, cut into 8 slices

4 onion rolls, split, buttered
    and toasted
8 slices boiled ham, warmed
4 to 8 eggs, poached
Becky's Blender Hollandaise
    (see page 102)
Paprika (optional)

In a large skillet, cook spinach in butter 2 minutes. Sprinkle with salt and pepper; separate into 4 mounds. Sauté tomato slices lightly, until just heated through, adding additional butter if needed. Cover bottom half of each roll with 2 ham slices, 2 tomato slices and a mound of spinach. Top with 1 or 2 eggs; pour sauce over all. Sprinkle with paprika. Serve remaining roll half on the side. Serves 4.

When you prepare these next refrigerator recipes, you can have fresh-baked breads every day of the week.

MOTHER'S ANGEL BISCUITS

5 cups flour
1/4 cup sugar
1 1/2 teaspoons salt
1 teaspoon soda
3 teaspoons baking powder

1/2 cup vegetable oil
1 to 2 packages dry yeast
2 to 3 tablespoons warm water
2 cups buttermilk

Sift together flour, sugar, salt, soda and baking powder. Cut in oil until mixture is crumbly. Stir yeast into the water until dissolved. Add yeast mixture and buttermilk to flour mixture; stir to combine. Turn dough onto lightly floured surface; knead about 5 minutes. Place in greased covered bowl large enough to allow dough to expand. Turn dough once to grease both sides. Place in refrigerator and leave at least 24 hours before the first baking. When ready to bake, preheat oven to 450 degrees. Punch dough down with fist and squeeze off required number of biscuits. Place in lightly greased pan, turning once to grease all sides. No additional rising time is necessary. Bake 10 to 15 minutes. Yields approximately 50 biscuits.

TIP: Mother's Angel Biscuits may be refrigerated in airtight container up to 3 weeks.

RAISIN BRAN MUFFINS

1 (15-ounce) box raisin bran
   cereal
1 quart buttermilk
5 cups flour

1 cup vegetable oil
2 teaspoons soda
2 teaspoons salt
3 cups sugar

Preheat oven to 400 degrees. Combine all ingredients in large bowl; stir well. Fill well-greased muffin cups ¾ full. Bake 20 minutes or until golden brown. Yields approximately 60 muffins.

ANY-TIME BRAN MUFFINS

1½ cups sugar
½ cup shortening
2 eggs
2½ cups flour
2½ teaspoons soda
½ teaspoon salt

2 cups buttermilk
1 cup boiling water
1 cup wheat bran cereal flakes
¾ cup raisins or currants
2 cups shredded wheat bran
   cereal

Preheat oven to 400 degrees. Cream sugar and shortening thoroughly. Add eggs one at a time, beating well after each addition. Combine flour, soda and salt. Add to the sugar mixture alternately with buttermilk. Mix until smooth. Meanwhile, pour boiling water over the wheat bran cereal flakes. Let stand until cereal has absorbed the water and cooled slightly. Blend cereal mixture into the batter. Add raisins or currants and remaining bran cereal. Mix thoroughly. Fill well-greased muffin cups ¾ full. Bake 20 minutes or until golden brown. Yields approximately 30 muffins.

TIP: These two delicious bran batters may be refrigerated in a covered container (a large wide-mouth jar is ideal) up to 5 weeks. Any time you need an excellent high-fiber muffin, simply dip the batter from the container (without stirring) and bake as directed.

These delightful coffee cakes are not only quickly prepared, but are ideally suited for a casual breakfast as they pull apart easily—good finger foods! And after trying these picture-perfect coffee cakes, you'll never resort to a convenience mix again.

CRUNCH BUBBLE CAKE

1½ cups granola
¾ cup brown sugar
1½ teaspoons cinnamon
2 (8-ounce) cans refrigerated
    biscuit dough

½ cup butter or margarine,
    melted

Preheat oven to 350 degrees. Combine granola, brown sugar and cinnamon in small bowl; mix well. Separate dough and cut each biscuit in half. Dip into melted butter; then roll in granola mixture, coating generously and pressing into dough. Layer in greased 12-cup bundt pan. Sprinkle with any remaining granola mixture; drizzle with remaining butter. Bake 30 minutes. Turn out immediately onto plate and serve warm. Serves 8 to 10.

HINT: Bake in an 8-inch cake pan when preparing half the recipe.

OVERNIGHT COFFEE CAKE

1 (25-ounce) package frozen
    dinner rolls (24 to package)
1 (3⅝-ounce) box regular
    butterscotch pudding mix
½ cup brown sugar

1 teaspoon cinnamon
¾ cup chopped pecans
6 tablespoons butter or
    margarine, melted

The night before serving, arrange rolls evenly in greased 12-cup bundt pan. Combine pudding mix, sugar, cinnamon and pecans. Sprinkle evenly over rolls. Drizzle melted butter over all. Cover and let set overnight. When ready to bake, preheat oven to 350 degrees; bake uncovered 30 minutes. Turn out immediately onto serving plate. Serves 6 to 8.

HINT: Don't let the pudding mix scare you off—Delicious!

QUICKIE STICKIE PECAN ROLLS

1 (12 count) package brown-
and-serve dinner rolls
4 tablespoons butter or
margarine

½ cup brown sugar
24 pecan halves

Preheat oven to 375 degrees. Place one roll in each of 12 well-greased muffin cups. Cut an x-shaped mark in top of each roll. Melt butter and sugar together over low heat. Mix well. Spoon mixture over the rolls. Tuck 2 pecan halves into cut on each roll. Bake 15 minutes or until browned. Yields 12 rolls.

ORANGE COCONUT BUNS

¼ cup butter or margarine
¼ cup brown sugar
¼ cup coconut
¼ cup sliced or slivered
almonds

½ cup orange marmalade
½ teaspoon ginger
1 (10-ounce) can refrigerated
flaky buttermilk biscuits

Preheat oven to 375 degrees. Combine butter, brown sugar, coconut and almonds in small oven-proof baking dish. Heat in oven until butter is melted. Remove from oven; divide evenly in 10 well-greased muffin cups. Combine marmalade and ginger. Divide dough into 10 biscuits. Spread about 2 teaspoons of the marmalade mixture on bottom of each biscuit. Place biscuits, marmalade side down, over coconut mixture. Bake 20 to 25 minutes or until golden brown. Cool 5 minutes. Loosen edges and invert onto serving plate. Yields 10 rolls.

Although the following recipes require some time and effort to prepare, the payoff to the hurried cook is the fact that all may be frozen and reheated when needed or refrigerated to provide effortless breakfasts for several days.

CHEESY SAUSAGE BUNS

1 package active dry yeast
1 cup warm water
2/3 cup instant nonfat dry milk
   powder
1 teaspoon salt
3 tablespoons sugar

1/4 cup melted butter or
   margarine
4 to 4 1/2 cups flour
1 egg
2 cups (8 ounces) shredded
   sharp Cheddar cheese

In a large bowl, dissolve yeast in warm water. Add milk, salt, sugar, butter and 2 cups flour. Beat until smooth. Add egg and beat well. Stir in cheese and enough remaining flour to make dough easy to handle. Turn dough onto floured surface; knead until smooth and elastic, about 10 minutes. Place in greased bowl; then turn so that greased side is up. Cover and let rise in warm place until doubled in bulk, about 1 1/2 hours. When doubled in size, punch dough down and divide into 18 balls. Flatten each; place 1 heaping tablespoon of Sausage Filling (see recipe below) into center. Shape into round buns and seal ends. Let rise on greased baking sheet until doubled, 35 to 45 minutes. When ready to bake, preheat oven to 375 degrees; bake 15 to 20 minutes or until golden brown. Cool 10 to 15 minutes before serving. Yields 18 buns.

Sausage Filling:
1/2 pound bulk sausage
1 cup chopped ripe olives

1/4 cup chopped walnuts

Brown sausage; drain well and cool to room temperature. Stir in olives and walnuts; combine well.

TIP: In addition to being a tasty on-the-run breakfast, try Cheesy Sausage Buns as a different companion to a full breakfast. The buns freeze beautifully and can be thawed to room temperature or reheated quickly in a microwave or conventional oven.

SWISS SAUSAGE TARTS

1¼ cups biscuit mix
¼ cup butter or margarine,
   softened
2 tablespoons boiling water
½ pound bulk sausage, cooked
   and drained
½ cup light cream

1 egg
2 tablespoons thinly sliced
   green onions
¼ teaspoon salt
½ cup (2 ounces) shredded
   Swiss cheese

Preheat oven to 375 degrees. Combine biscuit mix and butter. Add boiling water; mix vigorously until soft dough forms. Press 1 level tablespoon dough on bottom and up sides of 12 well-greased muffin cups. Divide sausage evenly among cups. Beat cream and egg; stir in onions and salt. Spoon about 1 tablespoon into each cup; sprinkle each with cheese. Bake until edges are golden brown and centers are set, about 25 minutes. Yields 12 tarts.

TIP: These tasty tarts can be frozen and reheated. Wrap in foil and bake at 300 degrees 20 to 25 minutes.

QUICHE LORRAINE TARTS

1 cup butter or margarine,
   softened
2 (3-ounce) packages cream
   cheese, softened
2 cups flour
1 tablespoon poppy seeds
1⅓ cups shredded Swiss cheese
10 slices bacon, fried crisp and
   crumbled

⅓ cup sliced green onions
4 eggs, beaten
1⅓ cups sour cream
1 teaspoon salt
1 teaspoon Worcestershire
   sauce

Preheat oven to 350 degrees. Combine butter, cream cheese, flour and poppy seeds; blend until smooth. Press about 2 tablespoons dough into 24 muffin cups (no need to grease). Combine Swiss cheese, bacon and green onion. Place approximately 2 tablespoons into each muffin cup. Combine eggs, sour cream, salt and Worcestershire sauce; pour 2 generous tablespoons into each muffin cup. Bake 20 to 25 minutes or until knife inserted in center comes out clean. Let tarts cool slightly before popping out of pans. Yields 24 tarts.

HINT: These freeze beautifully and can be reheated in 325 degree oven in 10 to 15 minutes. No need to thaw first.

MEXICAN MUFFINS

1 (11-ounce) can refrigerated
   buttermilk biscuits
1 cup (4 ounces) shredded
   Monterey Jack cheese
½ pound Chorizo (Mexican-style
   sausage)
⅛ cup chopped green onion

4 eggs, lightly beaten
¼ cup milk
½ teaspoon salt
¼ teaspoon red pepper sauce
5 green olives, halved
Cayenne pepper

Preheat oven to 375 degrees. On a lightly floured board, roll each biscuit to 5½-inch circle. Pat dough into 10 lightly-greased custard or muffin cups so that dough comes just to top of cups. Sprinkle 1 tablespoon cheese into each cup. Remove sausage from casing; cook with onion in skillet until onion is tender. Drain very well. Mix eggs, milk, salt and hot sauce with a fork or wire whisk. Divide sausage evenly among cups, pressing down gently. Pour egg mixture evenly among cups, allowing to soak down around sausage. Bake 25 minutes or until wooden pick inserted in center comes out clean. Sprinkle each cup with about ½ tablespoon remaining cheese; top with olive half. Bake 1 minute or until cheese melts. Sprinkle with cayenne pepper. Yields 10 muffins.

HINT: If Chorizo is not available, substitute pork sausage.

TRY THIS: For your next brunch, try any of the preceding muffin or tart recipes as your hors d'oeuvre. Utilizing miniature muffin cups, use approximately 2 teaspoons of dough (or ½ biscuit) for the crust, 2 teaspoons of filling, and 1 tablespoon of the custard liquid. Bake as directed.

BREAKFAST CUSTARD

2 eggs
2 cups milk
⅓ cup sugar

⅛ teaspoon salt
½ teaspoon vanilla extract
Ready-to-eat unsweetened cereal

Preheat oven to 350 degrees. In a small bowl, beat eggs with milk, sugar, salt and vanilla. Divide into five 6-ounce or three 10-ounce ungreased baking dishes. Sprinkle each with 3 or 4 tablespoons of your favorite dry cereal. Place baking dishes in shallow pan; pour hot water to ½-inch level around dishes. Bake 35 minutes or until knife inserted in center comes out clean. Cover and refrigerate until ready to serve. Serves 3 to 5.

JUDY'S MORNING GLORY PIE

2 cups cottage cheese
3 eggs, lightly beaten
²/₃ cup sugar
2 tablespoons flour

1 teaspoon orange peel
1 tablespoon orange juice
¼ teaspoon orange flavoring

Preheat oven to 350 degrees. Beat cottage cheese until almost smooth. Add remaining ingredients; stir until well blended. Pour into cooled crust (see recipe below); bake 45 to 50 minutes or until knife inserted in center comes out clean. Chill and serve with fresh fruit. Serves 6.

Crust:
1³/₄ cups flour
¼ teaspoon salt
¹/₃ cup vegetable oil

½ cup quick or old-fashioned
   oats, uncooked
Up to 6 tablespoons cold milk

Preheat oven to 450 degrees. Sift flour and salt together. Cut in oil until mixture resembles coarse crumbs. Stir in oats. Sprinkle milk by table-spoons over mixture, stirring with a fork after each addition until dampened. Press into bottom and halfway up sides of greased 8-inch square baking dish. Bake 10 to 12 minutes. Cool.

TIP: Pie can remain in refrigerator up to one week, providing a quick, nutritious week's worth of breakfasts for someone on the run!

OVERNIGHT FRUIT COMPOTE

1 (12-ounce) package mixed
   dried fruits
½ cup sugar
3 tablespoons lemon juice

2 teaspoons grated orange or
   lemon peel
3 sticks (3 inches each)
   cinnamon, broken

Thoroughly wash and drain fruit. Place in covered casserole or jar large enough to allow for expansion of fruits. Cover with boiling water; stir in sugar, lemon juice, peel and cinnamon. Add more sugar if sweeter fruit is desired. Cover container. Refrigerate at least 48 hours before serving to allow fruits to soften and flavors to blend. Serves 5 to 6.

NOTE: Compote may remain in refrigerator up to 2 weeks.

Who said you can't treat yourself to pancakes any day of the week? These toaster versions make a lazy-day specialty possible on even the busiest of mornings.

TOASTER OATMEAL PANCAKES

1½ cups uncooked rolled oats
2 cups milk
1 cup flour
2 teaspoons baking powder
1 teaspoon salt

2 tablespoons brown sugar
3 eggs, lightly beaten
4 tablespoons butter or
   margarine, melted

Place oats in deep bowl; stir in milk. Let stand until milk is almost absorbed, about 30 minutes. Sift flour with baking powder and salt. Stir in brown sugar and mix well. Add eggs to oat mixture; mix well. Sprinkle flour mixture over oats; add butter. Stir until just combined; do not overbeat. Lightly grease griddle or heavy skillet; heat slowly to medium-high. Use ¼ cup batter for each pancake. Cook until bubbles form on surface and edge becomes dry. Turn; cook 2 minutes longer or until nicely browned on underside. Serve hot with syrup. Yields sixteen 4-inch pancakes.

FREEZER BUTTERMILK PANCAKES

3 eggs
1 cup sifted flour
3 teaspoons baking powder
½ teaspoon salt
2 teaspoons sugar

1 teaspoon brown sugar
½ cup buttermilk
2 tablespoons butter or
   margarine, melted

In a large bowl, beat eggs with rotary beater at high speed until light and fluffy, about 2 minutes. Combine flour, baking powder, salt and white sugar. Sift into eggs. Add brown sugar; beat until smooth. Stir in buttermilk and butter until just combined; do not overbeat. Cook as directed for Toaster Oatmeal Pancakes. Serve hot with sour cream, syrup and assorted preserves. Yields eight 4-inch pancakes.

TO PREPARE IN ADVANCE: Cool oatmeal or buttermilk pancakes on wire rack. Wrap individually in foil and freeze flat. To re-heat: Unwrap desired number of pancakes. Place in toaster until heated through. (A second toasting may be necessary.)

Although preparation time is required for these next recipes, the beauty for the busy cook or hostess is that it occurs several hours—or even the day—before. When it's time to prepare the meal, simply pop these entrées into the oven and you're well on your way to a quick breakfast for even the heartiest of appetites!

SWISS CUSTARD RAMEKINS

Softened butter or margarine
2 slices bread
2 eggs, lightly beaten
1 cup light cream or milk
¼ cup dry white wine

⅛ teaspoon salt
⅛ teaspoon dry mustard
1½ cups (6 ounces) shredded
   Swiss cheese
2 green onions, thinly sliced

Spread butter on both sides of bread. Place in 2 well-greased individual baking dishes (about 1-cup size). Combine eggs, cream or milk, wine, salt and mustard. Evenly distribute cheese over bread; pour egg mixture over all. Sprinkle with onion. Cover and chill at least 2 hours or overnight. When ready to bake, preheat oven to 350 degrees. Bake uncovered 20 to 25 minutes or until custard is set when jiggled. Serves 2.

DOUBLY CHEESY STRATA

8 slices bread, crusts removed
2 cups (8 ounces) shredded mild
   Cheddar cheese
2 cups (8 ounces) shredded
   sharp Cheddar cheese

6 eggs, beaten
3 cups milk
¾ teaspoon dry mustard
Dash salt
Dash cayenne pepper

Cut bread into ½-inch cubes. Alternate layers of bread and cheeses in well-greased 2-quart soufflé dish or casserole. Combine eggs, milk, mustard, salt and cayenne; pour over bread and cheese. Cover and refrigerate overnight. When ready to bake, preheat oven to 350 degrees. Bake uncovered 1 hour or until firm in center and browned. Serves 4 to 6.

SAUSAGE AND EGG BRUNCH BAKE

2 cups herb croutons
1 pound bulk sausage, cooked
    and well drained
4 eggs, lightly beaten
2½ cups milk

1 teaspoon dry mustard
1½ cups (6 ounces) shredded
    Cheddar cheese
1 (10¾-ounce) can cream of
    mushroom soup

Line bottom of greased 9x13-inch glass baking dish with croutons. Cover with sausage. Combine eggs, milk, mustard, cheese and soup. Pour over sausage. Run a knife cross-wise through mixture as you would to marble cake batter. Cover and refrigerate overnight. When ready to bake, preheat oven to 325 degrees. Bake uncovered 1 hour and 15 minutes or until firm in center and brown on top. Let stand 5 minutes before cutting into squares. Serves 8.

SIMPLY CHEESY EGGS

4 English muffins, split,
    buttered and toasted
8 slices cooked Canadian bacon
8 eggs, poached
1½ cups pasteurized process
    cheese spread

Milk
Paprika
Snipped chives

Arrange muffin halves in greased 9x13-inch baking dish; top each with a bacon slice and egg. Cover and refrigerate. When ready to serve, preheat oven to 350 degrees. In a saucepan, combine cheese with just enough milk to liquify cheese (up to ¼ cup). Heat thoroughly. Pour cheese sauce over eggs. Bake uncovered 20 minutes. Sprinkle with paprika and snipped chives. Serve immediately. Serves 4 to 8.

The problem with most souffles is that the timing is too precise for an involved hostess or busy cook. The following recipes overcome this challenge and make the most elegant of entrées possible on any occasion.

FROZEN CHEDDAR SOUFFLÉ

2 tablespoons butter or
  margarine
¼ cup flour
½ teaspoon salt
¼ teaspoon pepper

¼ teaspoon dry mustard
1 cup milk
1½ cups (6 ounces) shredded
  sharp Cheddar cheese
6 eggs, separated

Melt butter in medium-size saucepan; remove from heat. Stir in flour, salt, pepper and mustard. Gradually stir in milk until smooth. Return to heat; continue cooking and stirring until mixture thickens and bubbles, about 1 minute. Stir in cheese until melted. Remove from heat and let cool. Beat egg whites in large bowl until stiff. Beat egg yolks well in a small bowl. Pour a little cooled cheese mixture into egg yolks, blending thoroughly. Pour egg yolk mixture into remaining cheese mixture; blend thoroughly. Fold cheese mixture into egg whites until no streaks of white or yellow remain. Pour into 6 well-buttered 10-ounce soufflé or custard cups. Cover tightly with foil or plastic wrap; freeze. When ready to serve, preheat oven to 350 degrees. Place frozen soufflés in oven and bake 40 minutes or until puffed and golden. Serves 6.

VARIATION: For FROZEN SWISS SOUFFLÉ, substitute 1 tablespoon snipped chives for dry mustard and 2 cups (8 ounces) shredded Swiss cheese for the Cheddar.

LAZY DAY CHEESE SOUFFLÉ

½ cup butter or margarine
½ cup sifted flour
1½ teaspoons salt
½ teaspoon paprika
Dash cayenne pepper or red
    pepper sauce

2 cups milk
2 cups (8 ounces) shredded or
    diced sharp Cheddar cheese
8 eggs, separated

Preheat oven to 475 degrees. Melt butter in top of a double boiler over boiling water. Add flour, salt, paprika and cayenne or pepper sauce. Mix well. Gradually stir in milk. Cook, stirring constantly, until sauce thickens. Add cheese; stir until melted. Remove from heat. Beat egg yolks until light. Gradually pour egg yolks into cheese sauce, stirring constantly. Wash beaters. Beat egg whites until stiff but not dry. Fold cheese sauce into egg whites until thoroughly blended. Pour mixture into greased and floured 10-inch soufflé dish. Bake 10 minutes. Reduce temperature to 400 degrees; bake 25 minutes longer. Let cool briefly before serving. Serves 4 to 6.

TO PREPARE IN ADVANCE: The prepared soufflé may be refrigerated up to 3 hours before baking. Remove from refrigerator about 20 minutes before placing in the preheated oven. Bake as directed.

PUFFED CHEESE CASSEROLE

8 slices day old whole grain
    bread, crusts removed
1½ cups (6 ounces) shredded
    sharp Cheddar cheese
3 eggs
⅛ teaspoon paprika

2 cups milk
Instant minced onions
Parsley
2 tablespoons grated Parmesan
    cheese

Cut bread into small cubes. Place in buttered 1-quart casserole or soufflé dish. Sprinkle Cheddar cheese on top of bread. Beat eggs with paprika. Add milk and combine well. Sprinkle generous amount of onions and then parsley on top of the cheese; add liquid to casserole. Sprinkle Parmesan cheese over all. Cover and let stand at least one hour or overnight. When ready to bake, preheat oven to 350 degrees. Bake uncovered 1 hour or until puffed and deep golden brown. Serves 4.

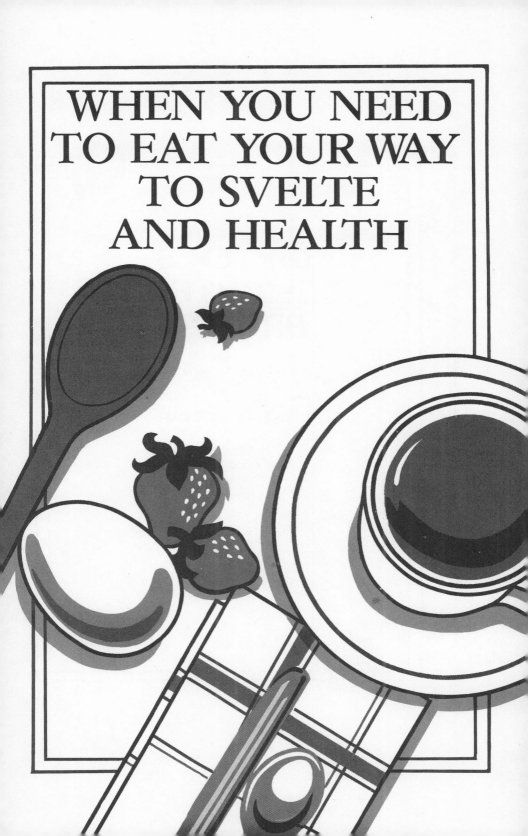

WHEN YOU NEED TO EAT YOUR WAY TO SVELTE AND HEALTH

DIETER'S DELIGHTFUL BRUNCH

Entrée
Baked Eggs Rockefeller

Vegetable
Italian Broiled Tomatoes

Fruit
Dieter's Fruit Delight

Bread

Variety of Egg-Free Muffins
Skinny Berry Preserves

Beverage
Coffee   Tea

Dieting is one of the best possible reasons to eat a good breakfast. A well-balanced meal "breaks the fast" between dinner and lunch, provides the nutrients and calories needed and utilized all day, and shores up your will power!

BAKED EGGS ROCKEFELLER

½ cup chicken bouillon
1 teaspoon instant minced onion
1 clove garlic, minced
1 (10-ounce) package frozen chopped spinach

¼ teaspoon monosodium glutamate (MSG)
¼ teaspoon thyme
Salt and pepper to taste
4 eggs

Preheat oven to 325 degrees. Combine bouillon, onions and garlic in a medium saucepan; bring to a boil. Add spinach; lower heat and simmer until tender, about 10 minutes. Drain. Season with MSG (optional), thyme, salt and pepper. Carefully break eggs into 2 well-greased individual baking dishes. Top with spinach mixture, covering eggs completely. Bake 12 to 15 minutes or until eggs are set as desired. Serves 2.

ZUCCHINI OMELETTE

1 medium onion, thinly sliced
1 clove garlic, crushed
2 tablespoons diet margarine
2 pounds zucchini, coarsely grated
1½ teaspoons salt

¼ teaspoon pepper
2 eggs
½ cup skimmed milk
½ cup grated Parmesan cheese
Paprika

Preheat oven to 350 degrees. In a large skillet, sauté onion and garlic in melted margarine until golden. Remove garlic; add zucchini, salt and pepper. Cover and simmer 5 to 7 minutes or until zucchini is fork-tender. Beat together eggs, milk and cheese. Combine zucchini and egg mixtures. Pour into greased 1½-quart shallow casserole or oven-proof skillet. Sprinkle with paprika. Bake 20 minutes or until firm. Dust lightly with additional Parmesan cheese if desired. Serve immediately. Serves 6.

NOTE: This omelette is not only low in calories with about 140 calories per serving, but it gets maximum mileage out of 2 eggs.

SLIMMER SPANISH OMELETTE

4 eggs   Pepper to taste
1 tablespoon water

Preheat broiler. Blend eggs, water and pepper in small bowl with fork. Place greased 9-inch oven-proof skillet over moderate-high heat until very hot. Immediately pour eggs all at once into skillet. Allow to set 8 to 10 seconds. Using a spatula, lift a portion of omelette; tilt pan, allowing uncooked portion to run underneath. Place under broiler and cook until omelette is doubled in size (it really will!) about 2 minutes. Slide omelette onto serving plate; fill with hot Spanish Sauce (see recipe below) and fold in half. Garnish with additional sauce. Serves 2—approximately 170 calories per serving.

Spanish Sauce:
2 tablespoons chopped onion   ¼ teaspoon salt
2 tablespoons chopped green   ⅛ teaspoon pepper
   pepper   ⅛ teaspoon cumin
1 (8-ounce) can tomato sauce

Combine all ingredients in saucepan. Bring to boil; cover and simmer 20 minutes or until thickened.

NOTE: You'll love this pretty and zesty omelette even if you're not on a diet. And this easy method of preparing omelettes is almost foolproof—try it with other fillings!

ALL-IN-ONE CASSEROLE

1 slice bacon, diced
½ small tomato, diced
1 green onion, thinly sliced
1 1-inch cube cheese, shredded
1 teaspoon chopped parsley

2 tablespoons diced boiled
   potatoes
1 egg
Pinch oregano
Salt and pepper to taste

Preheat oven to 350 degrees. Fry bacon until crisp. Add tomato and onion; cook 1 minute over medium heat. Remove to bowl with slotted spoon. Add cheese, parsley and potatoes to bacon mixture. Beat the egg, oregano, salt and pepper. Fold egg mixture into potato and bacon mixture; place in small greased casserole. Set casserole in a pan filled with ½-inch hot water. Bake 25 minutes or until set. Serve hot. Serves 1 for approximately 230 calories.

HINT: This fabulous combination makes an excellent one-dish breakfast and may be easily increased to serve any number. The bacon and vegetable mixture may be prepared the night before and the eggs added immediately before baking. So there's no excuse for not sticking to your diet!

ITALIAN BROILED TOMATOES

3 medium-size tomatoes
Salt and pepper to taste
¼ teaspoon dried oregano or
   basil

2 tablespoons low-calorie Italian
   salad dressing

Preheat broiler. Core tomatoes and cut in half cross-wise. Make shallow crisscross cuts on surface of tomatoes. Season cut surfaces with salt and pepper. Sprinkle with oregano or basil; drizzle with salad dressing. Broil, cut side up, 3 inches from heat 5 minutes or until heated through. Serves 3 to 6.

SKINNY BERRY PRESERVES

1½ teaspoons unflavored gelatin
2 tablespoons cold water
3 cups crushed or puréed
    berries

1 cup sugar substitute
Food coloring

Combine gelatin and water in small saucepan; heat, stirring constantly until gelatin is dissolved. Add berries. Bring to a boil over medium heat, stirring constantly. Reduce heat and simmer 2 minutes. Add sugar substitute and food coloring. Pour into jars; cover and refrigerate. Yields approximately 2½ cups of preserves, with each tablespoon containing about 4 calories.

VARIATION: Try strawberries, blueberries, raspberries, cherries or blackberries—fresh, canned or frozen. With no sugar added, of course!

DIETER'S FRUIT DELIGHT

1 (20-ounce) can pineapple
    chunks, no sugar added
2 small bananas
3 oranges, pared, sliced and
    seeded

½ pound seedless green grapes,
    cut in half
1 cup lemon-lime low-calorie
    carbonated beverage

Drain pineapple, reserving juice. Slice bananas on the bias into the reserved juice; remove with slotted spoon. Cut oranges into bite-size pieces. Layer pineapple, bananas, oranges and grapes in large salad bowl. Chill thoroughly. Just before serving, slowly pour chilled beverage over fruit and toss. Yields 5 cups.

BEAUTIFUL BERRY BOWL

1 (1-pound) can water-packed
    pitted tart red cherries
½ cup sugar substitute
1 tablespoon cornstarch
Dash salt

1 tablespoon lemon juice
4 drops red food coloring
Dash bitters (optional)
1 pint fresh strawberries, halved

Drain cherries, reserving juice. Add water to cherry juice to make 1½ cups. Blend sugar substitute, cornstarch, salt and cherry juice mixture. Cook, stirring until thickened and bubbly. Add lemon juice, food coloring, bitters and fruits. Chill thoroughly. Top with unflavored yogurt if desired. Serves 6.

SKINNY POPPY SEED DRESSING

2 teaspoons mayonnaise
2 tablespoons buttermilk

1 tablespoon sugar substitute
¼ teaspoon poppy seeds

Place all ingredients in small jar and shake well. Place in refrigerator overnight. Shake again before serving over your favorite fruits. Serves 1.

STRAWBERRY YOGURT

1 cup fresh or frozen
   strawberries
1 tablespoon lemon juice

1 tablespoon honey
½ cup unflavored yogurt

Wash and hull fresh strawberries or thaw frozen ones and use immediately. Mix lemon juice and honey; stir in yogurt. To serve, gently fold strawberries into yogurt mixture or pour mixture over strawberries in serving dish. Serves 1.

BANANA YOGURT

1 ripe banana, mashed
1 cup unflavored yogurt

Sugar substitute to taste
Cinnamon or instant coffee

Combine banana, yogurt and sugar substitute. Spoon into two dessert dishes; place in freezer about 30 minutes. Sprinkle with cinnamon or instant coffee before serving. Serves 2.

The following recipes meet—or can be easily adapted to meet—the breakfast requirements of many popular diets. As an added bonus, most are also quickly prepared and provide a single serving.

PEACH CRUNCH

2 canned peach halves, no
    sugar added
2 tablespoons reserved peach
    juice

½ cup unflavored yogurt
½ ounce bran or corn flakes
½ ounce toasted wheat germ

Thoroughly chill peaches and place cut side up in a dessert bowl. Stir yogurt into peach juice; spoon over fruit. Combine cereals and sprinkle over all. Serves 1.

BANANA "CHEESE CAKE"

⅓ cup ricotta cheese, chilled
Sugar substitute to taste

½ banana, peeled and sliced
1 slice bread

Combine cheese and sugar substitute; mix well. Fold banana slices into the cheese; spread on bread. Serves 1.

VARIATION: Substitute ½ cup strawberries or other berries for the banana.

BLUEBERRY PANCAKE

1 slice white bread, torn into
    pieces
1 egg
½ teaspoon vanilla

2 tablespoons skimmed milk
2 teaspoons sugar substitute
⅓ cup blueberries

Place bread in blender with egg, vanilla, milk and sugar substitute. Blend 1 minute. Fold in blueberries. Pour onto heated non-stick skillet. Brown on both sides. Serve with additional blueberries if desired. Serves 1.

BROILED CHEESE TOAST

1 slice whole grain bread	Sugar substitute to taste
1/3 cup low-fat cottage cheese	Cinnamon

Preheat broiler. Toast bread on one side. Combine cheese and sugar substitute, breaking up curds if possible. Turn toast over and spread with cheese mixture. Sprinkle with cinnamon. Broil until cheese is puffed and heated through. Serves 1.

PEACH QUICKIE

1/2 cup unflavored yogurt	1/4 teaspoon vanilla extract
1/2 cup canned sliced peaches, no sugar added	2 teaspoons low-calorie marmalade (optional)
2 teaspoons sugar substitute	1 medium egg

Combine all ingredients in blender; whirl at high speed until well blended. Pour over ice in tall glass and serve immediately. Serves 1.

STRAWBERRY SLENDER

1/2 cup evaporated skimmed milk	1 egg
1 cup frozen unsweetened strawberries (do not thaw)	Sugar substitute to taste
	Red food coloring (optional)

Combine all ingredients in blender; whirl at high speed until well blended. Serve immediately. Serves 1.

STRAWBERRY BREAKFAST PARFAIT

⅔ cup ricotta cheese
1 teaspoon vanilla flavoring
½ teaspoon butter flavoring

Sugar substitute
1 cup strawberries

Blend together cheese, flavorings and 2 teaspoons sugar substitute. Slice strawberries; sweeten to taste. Chill. Just before serving, fold strawberries into cheese mixture. Serves 1.

BREAKFAST BRAN COOKIES

1 ounce raisin or shredded
   wheat bran cereal
3 tablespoons non-fat dry milk
   powder

1 apple, grated
1 teaspoon vanilla extract
2 teaspoons sugar substitute
Cinnamon

Preheat oven to 350 degrees. Combine cereal, milk, apple, vanilla and sugar substitute. Drop teaspoons-full onto non-stick cookie sheet. Sprinkle with cinnamon. Bake 15 to 20 minutes. Yields 8 or 9 cookies. Serves 1.

BEAUTIFUL BREAKFAST BREADS

4 slices bread
1⅓ cups non-fat dry milk
   powder
1 teaspoon baking powder
8 tablespoons sugar substitute

4 eggs
1 teaspoon vanilla extract
Fruit or vegetable (see chart
   page 61)
Spices (see chart page 61)

Preheat oven to 350 degrees. Place bread in blender or food processor; process to make crumbs. Place crumbs in large bowl. Add powdered milk, baking powder and sugar substitute. Stir. Blend eggs and vanilla in blender or processor until fluffy. Fold egg mixture into bread crumbs; add one of the fruits or vegetables and spices from the chart. Combine well. Pour into four 4½ x 2½-inch non-stick loaf pans. Bake 30 to 45 minutes or until pick inserted in center comes out clean. Yields 4 loaves.

BREAD	FRUIT OR VEGETABLE	SPICES
Apple	4 medium apples, grated or 2 cups unsweetened applesauce	1 teaspoon apple pie spice and 1 teaspoon cinnamon
Banana	2 medium ripe bananas, mashed	2 teaspoons cinnamon
Pineapple	2 cups unsweetened crushed pineapple, drained	2 teaspoons cinnamon
Prune	16 medium prunes, cooked and diced	1½ teaspoons cinnamon and ⅛ teaspoon ginger
Blueberry	2 cups blueberries, drained (fresh or unsweetened canned or frozen)	2 teaspoons cinnamon
Cherry	2 cups cherries, drained (fresh or unsweetened canned or frozen)	2 teaspoons cinnamon
Cranberry	4 cups cranberries (fresh or unsweetened canned or frozen)	1 teaspoon cinnamon and ½ teaspoon allspice

NOTE: Add additional 2 tablespoons sugar substitute due to the tartness of the cranberries.

Carrot	2 medium carrots, grated, and 1 cup unsweetened crushed pineapple, drained	2 teaspoons cinnamon
Pumpkin	8 ounces cooked pumpkin	1 teaspoon cinnamon, 2 teaspoons pumpkin pie spice

NOTE: This is especially good with brown sugar substitute.

Zucchini	2 cups grated fresh zucchini	1 teaspoon cinnamon, ¼ teaspoon nutmeg and ¼ teaspoon cloves

NOTE: *Each loaf not only makes a complete diet breakfast, but can easily be frozen and re-warmed for a quick, mobile breakfast.*

The need to eat your way to health may be due to an illness, an allergic reaction, a preventative measure—or simply the desire to feel the best you can. Whatever your motivation, these next recipes are a delicious way to reach your goal.

GOLDEN SCRAMBLED TOFU

2 green onions, minced
2 tablespoons vegetable oil
½ teaspoon salt
½ teaspoon tumeric
1 cup tofu, well drained and
   mashed

1 or 2 teaspoons chicken
   bouillon granules
Garlic powder to taste
Dill weed

In a small skillet, sauté onion in oil until limp and transparent. Blend in salt and tumeric; add the tofu, scrambling to heat through. Sprinkle with bouillon and garlic powder. Mix thoroughly. Remove to plate and sprinkle with dill weed. Serves 2.

SPINACH OMELETTE

6 egg whites
½ cup frozen chopped spinach,
   thawed and drained

1 tablespoon mayonnaise
2 drops yellow food coloring
Salt and pepper to taste

Whip egg whites until frothy. Stir in spinach, mayonnaise, food coloring, salt and pepper. Pour egg mixture into heated non-stick skillet; cook until lightly set. Fold over and serve immediately. Serves 2. Omelette is both low in calories and in cholesterol.

TIP: Omelette is light and fluffy and should be handled gently. And even if you're not health conscious, this omelette is a delicious way to dispose of left-over egg whites—and why not experiment with the basic recipe, using other vegetables, cheese or meats?

Although there are many good recipes for granola, these next recipes are especially good, crammed with fiber and nutrition. And the last one has the added advantage of being the chief ingredient of an energy-packed breakfast bar. Serve it with fruit and milk for a well-balanced start for the day.

APPLE CINNAMON GRANOLA

5 cups oats
1 cup coconut
1 cup finely chopped cashews
1/2 cup wheat germ
1 teaspoon cinnamon

1/2 cup honey
1/3 cup vegetable oil
1 teaspoon vanilla extract
1/2 cup diced dried apples
1 tablespoon brown sugar

Preheat oven to 350 degrees. Spread oats on large ungreased pan; bake 10 minutes. Remove to large bowl. Add coconut, nuts, wheat germ and cinnamon. Stir. Add honey, oil and vanilla; combine thoroughly. Spread on pan; bake 30 minutes stirring occasionally. Remove from oven. Combine apples and brown sugar; add to granola. Store in covered container. Yields approximately 8 cups.

DO-YOUR-OWN-THING-GRANOLA

1 cup whole wheat flour
4 cups rolled oats
1 cup wheat germ
2 cups bran
1/2 cup sesame seeds

1/2 cup vegetable oil
1 cup water
1 teaspoon salt
3 cups "trail mix"

Preheat oven to 300 degrees. Combine flour, oats, wheat germ, bran, sesame seeds, oil, water and salt. Spread on large pan; bake 45 minutes. Stir once during baking. Turn off oven and add "trail mix". Let granola remain in oven until cooled and dry. Store in covered container. Yields approximately 12 cups.

VARIATION: Instead of "trail mix" try any combination of sunflower seeds, peanuts, cashews, almonds, chopped dates or raisins.

HONEY COCONUT GRANOLA

5 cups rolled oats
3 cups coconut
1 cup coarsely chopped walnuts,
   pecans or almonds
1 cup wheat germ
1/2 cup sesame seeds

1/2 cup sunflower seeds
1/2 teaspoon salt
3/4 cup honey
1/2 cup vegetable oil
2 teaspoons vanilla extract
1 cup chopped dates or raisins

Preheat oven to 350 degrees. In a large bowl, thoroughly combine oats, coconut, nuts, wheat germ, sesame seeds, sunflower seeds and salt. Heat honey, oil and vanilla in small saucepan. Pour over dry ingredients, stirring to coat well. Mix in dates or raisins. Spread mixture no more than 1/2-inch deep in shallow baking pan(s). Bake until lightly browned, about 30 minutes. Stir frequently to avoid overbrowning. Cool and store in tightly covered container(s). Yields approximately 12 cups.

GRANOLA BREAKFAST BARS

3/4 cup melted butter or
   margarine
1/3 cup brown sugar
1 teaspoon vanilla extract

1/2 teaspoon salt
3 eggs
5 1/2 to 6 cups Honey Coconut
   Granola

Preheat oven to 400 degrees. Combine butter and sugar in large mixing bowl; blend well. Add vanilla, salt and eggs; beat until smooth. Stir in granola. Turn into well-greased 9x13-inch baking pan; gently press down. Bake 16 to 20 minutes. Cool completely before slicing. Yields 32 to 40 squares.

APRICOT HEALTH LOAF

1 cup diced fresh or dried
   apricots
1 2/3 cups water
3 cups whole wheat pastry flour
5 tablespoons non-fat dry milk
   powder

4 teaspoons baking powder
1/4 teaspoon soda
1 1/2 teaspoons salt
1 cup sugar
3 tablespoons vegetable oil

Preheat oven to 350 degrees. If dried apricots are used, cover with boiling water until softened. If fresh fruit is used, use 1 cup hot water and 2/3 cup cold water. Sift flour with powdered milk, baking powder, soda and salt. Add sugar and oil to flour mixture. Blend in apricot mixture; pour into greased 9x5-inch loaf pan. Bake 55 minutes. Yields 1 loaf.

EGG-FREE MUFFINS

2 cups sifted flour
1/4 cup sugar
1/2 teaspoon salt
2 teaspoons baking powder

3/4 teaspoon soda
1 cup buttermilk
3 tablespoons vegetable oil
1/2 teaspoon butter flavoring

Preheat oven to 400 degrees. Sift flour, sugar, salt, baking powder and soda together. Combine buttermilk, oil and flavoring. Add buttermilk mixture all at once to dry ingredients. Stir until well blended. Fill 12 greased and floured muffin cups 2/3 full. Bake 20 to 25 minutes or until lightly browned and firm to the touch. Yields 12 large muffins.

VARIATION: Substitute 1 cup whole wheat flour for 1 cup of the white flour. Add 2 tablespoons molasses to the liquid ingredients. And try adding 1/2 cup chopped dates, raisins or walnuts to either version.

Pancakes and waffles don't have to be "off limits" to the health conscious. The first two recipes are deliciously available to those on many restricted or allergy diets, while the next two satisfy the requirements of even a health "nut"!

ENERGIZED PANCAKES

2 egg whites
3/4 to 1 cup skimmed milk
1 tablespoon cooking oil
1 cup flour
1/4 cup toasted wheat germ

1 1/2 teaspoons baking powder
1/4 teaspoon salt
1/2 cup dry-curd or low-fat
    cottage cheese

Whip egg whites with a fork. Add 3/4 cup milk and oil; stir. Mix together flour, wheat germ, baking powder and salt; add to liquid ingredients. Beat until well blended. Stir in cottage cheese. Thin batter with remaining milk if required to obtain desired consistency. Cook on lightly-greased hot griddle until golden brown on both sides. Yields twelve 3-inch pancakes that are both low in calories and cholesterol.

INCREDIBLE PANCAKES

2 eggs
2 medium ripe bananas, peeled

2 teaspoons sugar or sugar
  substitute

In blender at low speed, blend all ingredients until smooth. (If desired, mash bananas first; then add remaining ingredients.) Pour batter by ¼ cup portions onto lightly greased hot griddle. Cook until edges of pancakes are browned; turn and cook other side until golden brown. Yields six 4-inch pancakes that are gluten-, milk- and wheat-free.

TIP: Pancakes are very light and fluffy and brown easily. Handle carefully.

OATMEAL-BLUEBERRY PANCAKES

1½ cups whole wheat flour
1 cup rolled oats
½ cup toasted wheat germ
2 teaspoons baking powder
½ teaspoon salt

4 tablespoons honey
2 cups milk
2 eggs
1 cup blueberries, rinsed and
  well-drained

In a large bowl combine flour, oats, wheat germ, baking powder and salt. Set aside. In a small bowl beat honey, milk and eggs until well blended. Stir into flour mixture. Gently fold in berries. Pour ¼ cup batter for each pancake onto lightly greased hot griddle. Cook until golden on both sides. Yields 16 pancakes.

CRISP WHOLE WHEAT WAFFLES

¾ cup whole wheat flour
¼ cup (scant) stone ground
  cornmeal
¾ teaspoon baking powder
½ teaspoon soda

½ teaspoon salt
2 tablespoons cooking oil
1 egg, beaten
1 cup buttermilk

Preheat waffle iron; grease lightly. Mix all ingredients well, adding more buttermilk if batter is too thick to pour easily. Pour into prepared waffle iron and cook until golden. Yields 4 waffles.

WHEN THE KIDS
WANT TO GET IN
ON THE ACT

MOM AND DAD'S
BREAKFAST IN BED

Entrée
Cheesy Egg Puff
Bacon-A-Different-Way

Bread
French Toast Waffles
Assorted Preserves

Vegetable
Hash Brown Bake

Fruit
Pat's Heavenly Hash

Beverage
Coffee   Milk
Assorted Juices

The kids are guaranteed to love these breakfast beauties. And many make good "starter" recipes for them to try—without wrecking havoc in the kitchen!

CHEESY EGG PUFF

4 eggs
1/4 cup milk
1 teaspoon salt

1/8 teaspoon pepper
4 ounces Cheddar or American
   cheese

Preheat oven to 350 degrees. Combine eggs, milk, salt and pepper in large bowl. Beat with a rotary beater until mixture is very foamy. Grease a glass 9x5-inch loaf pan thoroughly. Pour in egg mixture. Cut the cheese into small cubes; sprinkle over the egg mixture. Bake 30 minutes or until golden brown and puffy. Serve immediately. Serves 4.

BAKED EGGS

1 egg
1 tablespoon milk or cream
1 tablespoon cracker crumbs

1 tablespoon shredded sharp
   Cheddar cheese
Salt and pepper to taste

Preheat oven to 400 degrees. Grease muffin cup. Place egg in cup; top with milk or cream, crumbs and cheese. Sprinkle with salt and pepper. Bake 12 to 20 minutes until egg is set as desired. Serves 1.

VARIATION: To complete the entrée, circle the inside of each muffin cup with a partially cooked bacon strip before adding egg and proceeding as directed. As many eggs as required may be prepared at the same time.

SOUPED UP SCRAMBLE

1 (10¾-ounce) can Cheddar
   cheese soup
8 eggs, lightly beaten
Dash pepper

2 tablespoons butter or
   margarine
Snipped chives

Pour soup into bowl; stir until smooth. Add eggs and pepper; blend thoroughly. In a medium skillet, melt butter; pour in egg mixture and scramble over low heat until set. Sprinkle with chives. Serves 4 to 6.

APPLE CORNFLAKE CAKE

4 tablespoons butter or
    margarine
2½ cups cornflakes
½ cup brown sugar
1 teaspoon cinnamon

3 teaspoons grated lemon peel
5 to 6 sharp apples, cored,
    peeled and sliced
3 tablespoons lemon juice
½ cup hot apple juice

Preheat oven to 350 degrees. Melt butter in saucepan over low heat. Turn off heat and add cornflakes, stirring to coat well. Mix brown sugar, cinnamon and lemon peel in small bowl. Cover bottom of greased 8-inch square baking dish with ⅓ of the buttered cornflakes. Layer ½ of apples on top of cornflakes. Sprinkle ½ of sugar mixture over apples. Repeat layers, ending with cornflakes. Drizzle lemon juice over layers; pour apple juice slowly over all. Cover with foil and bake 10 minutes. Remove foil and continue baking 30 minutes more. Serves 4 to 6.

HINT: Try serving this "cake" with a scoop of cottage cheese for a quick, nutritious breakfast. And for extra nutrition, substitute 1 cup wheat germ for 1 cup cornflakes. For extra quickness, bake ahead of time and simply reheat uncovered in 350 degree oven for 10 minutes.

SPICED APPLE PANCAKE

3 tablespoons butter or
    margarine
2 apples, cored, peeled and
    sliced
Sugar
Cinnamon

Nutmeg
¼ cup milk
1 egg
¼ cup flour
Pinch salt
2 tablespoons cinnamon-sugar

Preheat oven to 450 degrees. Melt 2 tablespoons butter in a medium skillet. Cook apples until tender, about 10 minutes. Sprinkle apples generously with sugar, cinnamon and nutmeg. Keep warm. Beat milk and egg with a rotary beater. Beat in flour and salt; continue to beat until batter is very frothy. Melt remaining tablespoon butter in a medium oven-proof skillet. Pour in batter. Bake 12 minutes; prick bubbles on surface and spread with cooked apples. Sprinkle with cinnamon-sugar. Set under broiler 5 minutes to glaze. Divide equally and serve hot. Serves 2.

HINT: Especially good served with smoked pork chops—try it!

SLEEPYHEAD OATMEAL

2 cups old-fashioned rolled oats
1/2 cup chopped almonds
1 cup chopped raisins

1 teaspoon cinnamon
3 cups water

Combine oats, almonds, raisins and cinnamon. Mix well. Add water; stir to combine well. Cover and refrigerate overnight before serving. Yields 5 cups.

NOTE: Sleepyhead Oatmeal lasts well in the refrigerator and gets even better after 2 or 3 days. The oatmeal may be served cold with milk or yogurt, cottage cheese or fruit. Or it may be heated in a microwave oven on high for 2 minutes and served with cream and sugar.

FRENCH TOAST WAFFLES

1 egg, beaten
1/4 cup milk
2 tablespoons melted butter or
    margarine

1/8 teaspoon salt
6 slices bread

Combine egg, milk, butter and salt. Coat bread on both sides with batter. Toast on a hot waffle iron until golden brown. Serve with syrup, honey or preserves. Serves 3 to 4.

Not only can the kids make these sandwiches themselves—but you'll get no breakfast-time arguments when these palate-pleasing items are on the menu!

THE JAMES GANG'S CREAM CHEESE TOAST

4 slices bread
Cream cheese, softened
Preserves

1 egg
1/4 cup milk
Butter or margarine

Spread 2 slices bread generously with cream cheese and preserves. Top with remaining bread. Beat egg and milk together. Heat butter in large skillet. Dip sandwiches in egg mixture, coating on both sides. Sauté in butter until golden brown on both sides. Serves 2.

DEVILISHLY QUICK SANDWICHES

1 (4½-ounce) can deviled ham
2 English muffins, split and
   toasted

4 eggs, fried
4 slices American cheese

Preheat oven to 350 degrees. Spread deviled ham evenly on muffin halves; warm in oven. Top each muffin half with egg and cheese slice. Return to oven until cheese melts, about 10 minutes. Serves 2 to 4.

EGG McWALKER

1 bakery or hamburger bun
Mayonnaise or butter
1 egg, fried hard

1 slice American cheese
1 slice ham or luncheon meat
Salt and pepper to taste

Preheat broiler. Spread both halves of bun with mayonnaise or butter. While egg is frying, toast bun with cheese on one half and meat on the other. Place fried egg between bun halves. Sprinkle with salt and pepper; combine into sandwich. Serves 1.

SNAPPY CHEESE SANDWICHES

4 strips bacon
2 eggs, beaten
2 cups (8 ounces) shredded
   sharp Cheddar cheese

2 teaspoons Worcestershire
   sauce
4 slices bread, toasted lightly
   on both sides

Preheat broiler. Fry bacon 2 or 3 minutes until transparent. Drain on paper towels. Combine eggs, cheese and Worcestershire sauce. Spread on toasted bread. Cut bacon in half; place 2 pieces on each slice of toast. Broil 4 inches from flame until bacon is crisp and egg/cheese mixture is cooked and slightly puffed. May be served as open-faced sandwiches, serving 4. For increased mobility and heartiness, combine 2 slices into a single sandwich, serving 2.

COTTAGE CHEESE SANDWICHES

1 cup cottage cheese
1/4 cup chopped nuts
8 slices bread
2 eggs
2 tablespoons water

4 tablespoons butter or
   margarine
4 tablespoons brown sugar
   (optional)

Mix cottage cheese and nuts; spread on 4 slices bread. Cover with remaining slices. Beat eggs and water until well blended. Carefully dip sandwiches in egg mixture, coating both sides. Sauté in melted butter until golden brown on both sides. Sprinkle with brown sugar. Serves 4.

HAM AND CHEESE FRENCH TOAST SANDWICHES

3 eggs
3/4 cup milk
1 tablespoon sugar
1/4 teaspoon salt
8 slices bread, lightly buttered

4 slices cooked ham
4 slices Swiss or American
   cheese
Butter or margarine

Beat eggs, milk, sugar and salt with rotary beater just until combined. Top 4 pieces of bread with ham and cheese slices. Top with remaining bread; cut into quarters diagonally. Place in single layer in shallow baking dish. Pour egg mixture over all, covering completely. Cover and refrigerate overnight. Just before serving, sauté sandwiches in melted butter until golden on both sides and cheese is slightly melted. Serves 4.

These "toast toppers" are sure to become favorites in your house!

CHEDDAR-OLIVE SPREAD

1 cup chopped black olives
1 cup (4 ounces) shredded
    Cheddar cheese
½ cup mayonnaise

½ cup finely chopped green
    onions
1 teaspoon salt

Combine all ingredients and mix well. Store in covered container in refrigerator. Yields approximately 3 cups spread.

TO SERVE: Spread Cheddar-Olive Spread generously on English muffins. Bake in 350 degree oven 30 minutes or broil until cheese is melted. Serve open-faced or as a sandwich.

OR TRY THIS: After baking, quarter the muffins and serve as an hor d'oeuvre.

HONEY-PEANUT BUTTER HEALTH SPREAD

½ cup natural chunky peanut
    butter
½ cup toasted wheat germ

½ cup honey
3 tablespoons butter or
    margarine, softened

Combine all ingredients and mix well. Store in the refrigerator. Yields 1½ cups.

TO SERVE: Split and toast high-fiber English muffins. Spread Honey-Peanut Butter Health Spread on warm muffins. Yummy!

JOYCE'S PEANUT BUTTER AND JELLY SPREAD

1 cup grape jelly   ½ cup creamy peanut butter
1½ cups raisins

Place jelly in blender or food processor. Add raisins and process until raisins are puréed. Add peanut butter. Mix until blended. Cover tightly and store (no need to refrigerate). Yields 2 cups.

TO SERVE: Spread generously on slice of bread. Serve open-faced or as a sandwich.

HONEY BUTTER

½ cup butter or margarine,   1 cup honey
   softened

Blend butter and honey thoroughly. Store in refrigerator. Yields approximately 1½ cups or enough for about 16 pieces of toast.

TO SERVE: Lightly toast slices of bread on one side. Turn and spread the untoasted side with Honey Butter. Sprinkle with cinnamon. Place under broiler until golden.

"Breakfast in a glass" is a great way to start any child's day—it's quick, easy and nutritious. The endless tasty combinations also insure no more boring breakfasts! Try these next recipes for openers—and then let your creativity take over!

THE BASTROP BOYS' BIONIC BREAKFAST

1 cup skimmed or whole milk   1 teaspoon honey
1 egg
1 banana, peeled and broken
   into pieces

Place all ingredients in a blender; add 2 or 3 ice cubes if desired. Whip 1 minute until smooth; serve immediately. Serves 1.

75

LONG'S LANKY BREAKFAST DRINK

1 egg
¾ cup milk
1 small banana, peeled

2 tablespoons crushed pineapple
and its juice

Place all ingredients in blender; whirl until banana and pineapple are liquefied. Pour into tall glass; add more milk to fill glass if desired. Serves 1.

UP-AND-AT-'EM INSTANT BREAKFAST

1 banana, peeled and broken
into pieces
½ cup orange juice
½ cup milk

1 tablespoon honey
1 teaspoon wheat germ
1 egg

Place all ingredients in blender, adding 2 or 3 ice cubes if desired. Process 1 minute and serve immediately. Serves 1.

JUNE'S BEST EVER POTATOES O'BRIEN

1 (32-ounce) bag frozen
Potatoes O'Brien
1 (8-ounce) carton sour cream
1 (10¾-ounce) can potato soup
1 (10¾-ounce) can celery soup

1 cup milk
3 tablespoons instant minced
onion
1 (8-ounce) jar pasteurized
process cheese spread

Preheat oven to 350 degrees. Combine all ingredients and stir well. Spoon into greased 2½-quart casserole. Bake 1 hour. Serves 12.

HASH BROWN BAKE

1 (32-ounce) bag frozen hash
   brown potatoes, thawed
¾ cup butter or margarine,
   melted
½ cup chopped onion
1 (10¾-ounce) can cream of
   chicken soup

1 (8-ounce) carton sour cream
1 cup (4 ounces) shredded
   Cheddar cheese
2 cups crushed cornflakes

Preheat oven to 350 degrees. Combine potatoes, ½ cup butter, onions, soup, sour cream and cheese. Stir well. Spoon into greased 2½-quart casserole. Combine cornflakes and remaining butter. Sprinkle over potato mixture. Bake 50 minutes. Serves 12.

PAT'S HEAVENLY HASH

1 cup pineapple chunks
1 cup mandarin orange sections
1 cup shredded coconut

1 cup miniature marshmallows
1 cup sour cream

Combine all ingredients and chill thoroughly. Serves 4.

LULU'S SWEET FRUIT SALAD

1 (16-ounce) can sliced peaches,
   drained
1 (16-ounce) can pineapple
   chunks, undrained
1 (6-ounce) jar maraschino
   cherries, undrained

2 or 3 bananas, peeled and
   thinly sliced
1 (3¾-ounce) package instant
   vanilla pudding mix

Combine fruits; sprinkle pudding mix over all. Stir with wooden spoon. Cover and refrigerate overnight. Serves 8.

TOP OF THE MORN' AMBROSIA

¼ cup powdered sugar
1½ cups coconut
2 large oranges, seeded and
   sliced

3 bananas, peeled and thinly
   sliced
½ cup pineapple, drained

Combine sugar and coconut. Alternate layers of fruit in individual serving dishes. Sprinkle each layer with sugar/coconut mixture, reserving some for the top. Chill well before serving. Serves 4.

VARIATION: Substitute strawberries, grapes, peaches, apricots or cherries for the pineapple.

BROILED GRAPEFRUIT

1 grapefruit, cut in half
2 tablespoons honey
Salt

1 teaspoon butter or margarine
Garnish

Preheat broiler. Loosen each grapefruit section by cutting down and along either side of dividing membranes and around outer skin. Do not remove fibrous center. Sprinkle each half with 1 tablespoon honey. Sprinkle lightly with salt; dot each half with ½ teaspoon butter. Broil 4 inches from heat 8 to 10 minutes until fruit is heated through and lightly browned around edges. (Overcooking may cause bitter taste.) Garnish center of grapefruit halves with fresh berries, maraschino cherry or mint sprigs; serve immediately. Serves 2.

VARIATION: Try brown sugar, finely crushed peppermint candy or maple syrup in place of the honey. Surprisingly good!

WHEN YOU NEED SOMETHING TO GO WITH EVERYTHING

WEDDING BELL BRUNCH

Hors D'Oeuvre
Quiche Lorraine Tarts

Soup
Barbara's Fruit Soup

Entrée
Frozen Cheddar Soufflé   Frozen Swiss Soufflé
Crab Vermicelli

Vegetable
Orange-Almond Salad   Broccoli Surprise

Bread
Blueberry Muffins   Coffee Cake Muffins
Assorted Preserves   Cream Cheese

Beverage
Coffee   Champagne Punch
Served with Whipped
Cream and Assorted
Liqueurs

TEXAS HASH

2 (10¾-ounce) cans creamy
   chicken mushroom soup
1 large onion, diced
1 (8-ounce) package cream
   cheese, softened
1 pint sour cream
1 (32-ounce) bag frozen hash
   browns

1 cup (4 ounces) shredded
   Cheddar cheese
1 (8-ounce) package corn bread
   stuffing mix
½ cup butter or margarine,
   melted

Preheat oven to 350 degrees. Combine soup, onion, cream cheese, sour cream and hash browns. Place in greased 9x13-inch casserole. Sprinkle with cheese. Using rolling pin, crush stuffing mix until there are no large pieces. Combine stuffing mix with butter; sprinkle over top. Bake 45 minutes to 1 hour. Serves 12.

GERMAN FRIES

¼ cup shortening
2 potatoes, boiled, peeled and
   sliced

1 bunch green onions, sliced
Salt and pepper to taste
Parsley

Heat shortening in large heavy skillet. Add potatoes and sauté. Add onions, salt and pepper. When potatoes are brown and onions are limp, sprinkle with parsley. Serves 2.

SESAME HASH BROWNS

1 green onion, finely minced
4 tablespoons butter or
   margarine
¼ cup sesame seeds
4 potatoes, cooked, peeled and
   diced

1 teaspoon salt
½ teaspoon freshly ground
   pepper
¼ cup heavy cream
Parsley

Sauté onion in butter. Add sesame seeds and cook until lightly browned. Add potatoes, salt, pepper and cream. Cook, stirring occasionally until potatoes are golden brown. Sprinkle with parsley. Serves 4 to 6.

DOWN-HOME FRIED POTATOES

2 large yellow onions, chopped
½ cup butter or bacon fat
5 large potatoes, cooked, chilled
   and sliced

Seasoned salt
Freshly ground black pepper
Paprika
Chopped parsley

Sauté onions in ¼ cup hot fat until well browned. Remove onions from skillet; set aside and keep warm. Heat remaining fat in same skillet. Sauté unpeeled potatoes in the fat, turning to brown both sides. When almost cooked, return onions to skillet. Mix well. Season to taste with salt and pepper. Turn into bowl or place on serving plates; sprinkle with paprika and parsley. Serves 8.

CHEESE GARLIC GRITS

1 (6-ounce) package garlic and
   herb cheese, room
   temperature
1 egg, lightly beaten
4 tablespoons butter or
   margarine

¼ cup milk
Dash red pepper sauce
1 cup quick-cooking grits,
   cooked

Preheat oven to 375 degrees. Cut cheese into small pieces. Add cheese, egg, butter, milk and hot sauce to hot grits. Stir thoroughly until cheese is blended and butter is melted. Pour into greased 1½-quart baking dish. Bake 30 to 40 minutes or until golden brown and center is set. Serves 6.

SOUTHERN GRITS SOUFFLÉ

4 tablespoons butter or
   margarine
2 bunches green onions, thinly
   sliced
2½ teaspoons salt
4 cups (16 ounces) shredded
   sharp Cheddar cheese

2-3 dashes red pepper sauce
6 eggs, separated
2 cups quick-cooking grits,
   cooked

Preheat oven to 400 degrees. Stir butter, onions, salt, cheese, hot sauce and egg yolks into hot grits. Cool slightly. Beat egg whites until soft peaks form. Fold egg whites into grits mixture; pour into well-greased 2-quart casserole. Bake 40 minutes. Serves 12.

BROCCOLI SURPRISE

1 (14-ounce) can artichoke
  hearts, drained and
  quartered
1/2 cup butter or margarine,
  melted
1 (8-ounce) package cream
  cheese, softened

1 1/2 teaspoons lemon juice
2 (10-ounce) packages frozen
  chopped broccoli, cooked
  and drained well
Saltine cracker crumbs

Preheat oven to 350 degrees. Place artichokes on bottom of well-greased 1 1/2-quart casserole. Combine butter, cream cheese and lemon juice. Add broccoli to cream cheese mixture; pour over artichokes. Top with cracker crumbs. Bake 25 minutes. Serves 6.

BARBARA'S BROCCOLI BAKE

1/2 (10 3/4-ounce) can cream of
  mushroom soup
1/2 cup (2 ounces) shredded
  sharp Cheddar cheese
1 egg, beaten
1/2 cup mayonnaise

1 tablespoon grated onion
Salt and pepper to taste
1 (10-ounce) package frozen
  chopped broccoli, cooked
  and drained
1/2 cup cheese cracker crumbs

Preheat oven to 350 degrees. Combine soup, cheese, egg, mayonnaise, onions, salt and pepper. Add broccoli and mix well. Pour into greased 1-quart casserole; top with cracker crumbs. Bake 25 to 30 minutes. Serves 4.

CREAMED SPINACH

2 (10-ounce) packages frozen
  chopped spinach, cooked
  and drained well

1 cup sour cream
1 envelope dry onion soup mix

Preheat oven to 350 degrees. Combine all ingredients. Pour into well-greased 2-quart casserole. Bake 30 minutes. Serves 8.

TIP: The mixture may be refrigerated or frozen after the ingredients have been combined. Thaw to room temperature before baking as directed.

Baked tomatoes round out a breakfast menu beautifully. Use this recipe and then experiment. Try other combinations of herbs. Drizzle with salad dressings and top with your favorite cheese or seasoned bread crumbs. The result? Endless variations to complement any menu!

BAKED SAVORY TOMATOES

2 medium tomatoes, washed
    and dried
¼ teaspoon salt
¼ teaspoon rosemary

¼ teaspoon basil
2 teaspoons butter or
    margarine

Preheat oven to 350 degrees. Cut tomatoes in half using a sawtooth pattern if desired. In a small cup, mix salt, rosemary and basil. Sprinkle each tomato half with herb mixture; dot with butter. Place tomato halves in shallow baking dish; bake 20 minutes or until tomatoes are tender and heated through. Serves 2 to 4.

HOT SPINACH SALAD

1 (10-ounce) package fresh
    spinach
6 slices bacon
1 medium onion, chopped
    coarsely

¼ cup wine vinegar
Salt and pepper to taste
1 cup (4 ounces) shredded
    Swiss cheese

Preheat broiler. Wash and trim spinach; chop randomly. Thoroughly pat dry and place in greased 2-quart casserole. Cook bacon in large skillet until crisp. Drain on paper towels and crumble. Sauté onion in bacon grease until limp. Add vinegar to onion mixture and heat through. Sprinkle bacon over spinach; pour warm grease and onions over all. Toss to mix. Sprinkle with salt and pepper; top with cheese. Place under broiler until cheese melts and bubbles. Serves 4.

ORANGE-ALMOND SALAD

2 quarts chilled salad greens
4 slices bacon, fried crisp and
    crumbled
¼ cup sliced almonds

2 green onions, thinly sliced
1 (11-ounce) can mandarin
    orange segments, drained
    and chilled

Combine all ingredients in large salad bowl. Pour Dressing (see recipe below) over and toss. Garnish with additional almonds if desired. Serves 4 to 6.

Dressing:
¼ cup salad oil
2 tablespoons sugar
2 tablespoons vinegar

½ teaspoon salt
Dash red pepper sauce

Combine all ingredients in covered jar. Mix well and chill.

SALAD MEXICANA

1 head romaine lettuce torn into
    bite-size pieces
3 large oranges, chilled, peeled
    and seeded

2 large ripe avocados, chilled,
    peeled and seeded

Place lettuce (about 6 cups) in a large salad bowl. Chill thoroughly. Just before serving, cut each orange section into bite-size pieces. Slice the avocados. Arrange avocado and orange slices over the lettuce. Drizzle ⅓ to ½ cup Mexicana Lemon Dressing (see recipe below) over salad. Toss gently. Serves 6.

Mexicana Lemon Dressing:
¼ cup lemon juice
½ teaspoon salt
⅛ teaspoon pepper

¼ teaspoon sugar
¼ teaspoon dry mustard
½ cup salad oil

Combine lemon juice, salt, pepper, sugar and dry mustard in a small bowl. Beat well with a wire whisk. Pour in oil in a slow steady stream, beating until mixture is thick and creamy. Refrigerate in covered jar. Shake thoroughly before serving. Yields ¾ cup.

Providing a variety of interesting fruits can be a challenge, especially for winter-time menus. These next recipes meet that challenge. But don't forget about baked apples, broiled spiced peaches, canned or fresh apricots and figs, bananas with cream, grapefruit garnished with berries or sprig of mint, cooked dried fruits and frozen fruits combined with fresh bananas.

BARBARA'S FRUIT SOUP

4 cups pineapple juice
1/2 cup tapioca
4 cups orange juice
2 cups diced apples
1 cup crushed or chunk
    pineapple

2 cups chopped orange sections
2 cups green grape halves
Up to 1 cup sugar
Toasted coconut

Combine pineapple juice and tapioca in a large saucepan; let stand 5 minutes. Stir over low heat until tapioca becomes clear. Remove from heat and add orange juice. Cool. Add apples, pineapple, oranges and grapes. Taste and add sugar according to desired sweetness. Chill thoroughly. Garnish with coconut. Yields 15 cups.

SUMMER SPECIAL SALAD

1 medium cantaloupe, peeled
    and seeded
2 cups fresh or frozen
    blueberries, rinsed and
    drained

1/2 pound seedless green grapes,
    rinsed and cut in half

Cut cantaloupe into 6 wedges; place each on a salad plate. Divide blueberries and grapes evenly over cantaloupe. Cover with plastic wrap; chill until serving time. When ready to serve, spoon Summer Special Sauce (see recipe below) over fruit. Serve immediately. Serves 6.

Summer Special Sauce:
1 cup sour cream
1/3 cup brown sugar

1/4 teaspoon cinnamon

Mix all ingredients in small bowl; cover and refrigerate until ready to serve.

SHERRIED FRUIT SALAD

2 oranges, peeled and seeded
1 pint strawberries, hulled and
    sliced in half
2 bananas, peeled and sliced
1 (20-ounce) can pineapple
    chunks; drained (Reserve ¼
    cup juice for Sherry
    Dressing)

Lettuce

Cut oranges into bite-size pieces; combine fresh fruits and pineapple. Toss with Sherry Dressing (see recipe below). Serve on lettuce-lined salad plates or in dessert bowls. Serves 6.

Sherry Dressing:
1 egg
1 teaspoon cornstarch
¼ cup reserved pineapple juice
¼ cup sherry

¼ teaspoon salt
3 tablespoons lemon juice
3 tablespoons sugar
½ cup sour cream

Beat egg with cornstarch until cornstarch is dissolved. Add reserved pineapple juice, sherry, salt, lemon juice and sugar. Cook in top of a double boiler over hot water, stirring until thickened. Remove from heat. When cool, fold in sour cream and refrigerate until serving.

FROZEN AMBROSIA DELIGHT

1 (3-ounce) package cream
    cheese, softened
½ cup sifted powdered sugar
1 cup sour cream
⅓ cup frozen orange juice
    concentrate, thawed

½ cup whipping cream
1 (16-ounce) can fruit
    cocktail, drained
1 (11-ounce) can mandarin
    orange sections, drained
¼ cup flaked coconut, toasted

Beat together cream cheese and powdered sugar. Gradually beat in sour cream and orange juice concentrate. Whip cream; fold into cream cheese mixture. Add fruit cocktail and mandarin orange sections; stir gently to combine. Spread in 9-inch square glass baking dish. Freeze until firm. Let stand at room temperature about 10 minutes before serving. Serve on lettuce leaves if desired; sprinkle with coconut. Serves 8 to 10.

HONEY OF A FRUIT SALAD

3 bananas, peeled and sliced
2 grapefruit, sectioned with
    seeds and membrane
    removed
1 pint strawberries, hulled and
    cut in half

¾ cup Orange Honey Dressing
    (see recipe below)
Lettuce
Slivered almonds

Combine bananas, grapefruit sections and strawberries. Toss with salad dressing. Marinate in refrigerator at least 1 hour but not longer than 3. Drain and serve on lettuce. Garnish with slivered almonds and serve with additional dressing. Serves 6 to 8.

Orange Honey Dressing:
¼ cup frozen orange juice
    concentrate
1 tablespoon vinegar
4 tablespoons lemon juice
¼ cup honey

½ teaspoon dry mustard
½ teaspoon salt
¼ cup salad oil
2 teaspoons poppy seeds

Combine all ingredients in covered jar; shake to mix thoroughly.

CREAMY FRUIT SALAD

1 (20-ounce) can pineapple
    chunks, drained
1 (8¾-ounce) can sliced
    peaches, drained
1 (8¾-ounce) can pears, drained
1 (11-ounce) can mandarin
    orange sections, drained
½ cup sugar

½ cup coconut
2 cups miniature marshmallows
1 cup sour cream
2 bananas, peeled and sliced
1 pint strawberries, hulled and
    cut in half
Slivered almonds

Combine pineapple, peaches, pears and orange sections. Sprinkle with sugar; toss. Add coconut, marshmallows and sour cream; combine well. Chill. Just before serving, add bananas and strawberries. Serve on lettuce leaves or in dessert bowls; garnish with almonds. Serves 10.

WIDE AWAKE FRUIT SALAD

2 or 3 avocados   Lettuce
2 or 3 white or ruby red
   grapefruit

Just before serving, peel and slice avocados. Peel grapefruit; separate into sections, removing seeds and excess membrane. Alternate avocado slices and grapefruit sections in spoke pattern on individual lettuce-lined salad plates. Spoon Wide Awake Dressing (see recipe below) over fruit. Serves 6 to 8.

Wide Awake Dressing:
2 cups salad oil   2 teaspoons salt
1 to 1¼ cups sugar   2 teaspoons dry mustard
⅔ cup white wine vinegar   ¼ teaspoon dry tarragon
3 tablespoons finely minced   3 tablespoons poppy seeds
   green onion (white
   part only)

In a blender, combine all ingredients except poppy seeds; process until thickened. Add poppy seeds and blend quickly.

TO PREPARE AHEAD OF TIME: Omit lettuce and alternate avocado slices and grapefruit sections in shallow bowl. Pour dressing over; cover and refrigerate.

BAKED FRUIT COMPOTE

1 (13½-ounce) can pineapple   ½ cup brown sugar
   chunks, drained   2½ teaspoons tapioca
1 (16-ounce) can sliced   1 tablespoon butter or
   peaches, drained   margarine
1 (6-ounce) jar maraschino
   cherries, drained

Preheat oven to 350 degrees. Place fruits, sugar and tapioca in greased 2-quart casserole; stir gently to combine. Dot with butter. Cover and bake 35 minutes. Serves 4 to 6.

SPICED ICED FRUIT BOWL

2 (29-ounce) cans peach halves
1 (29-ounce) can pear halves
1/4 cup white vinegar
1/4 teaspoon salt
3/4 teaspoon whole allspice

1/2 teaspoon whole cloves
4 3-inch long cinnamon sticks
1 pound red or Ribier (black)
   grapes, halved and seeded

Drain syrup from peach and pear halves into 2-quart saucepan; stir in vinegar and salt. Tie allspice, cloves and cinnamon sticks in small square of cheese cloth; add to syrup mixture. Heat syrup and spice mixture to boiling over medium heat. Reduce heat to low; cover and simmer 10 minutes to blend flavors. Remove from heat; cool about 15 minutes. Combine fruits in large bowl. Pour syrup and spice mixture over fruit; toss to coat well. Cover and refrigerate at least overnight or up to 3 days, stirring occasionally. When ready to serve, discard cheese cloth bag. Serves 16.

The "Breads of Breakfast" could fill an entire book and most cookbooks include many good ones. The breads selected for this section—and those throughout the book—have special qualities: They're either uniquely breakfast; are prepared quickly and easily; or are just too delicious to omit!

LEMON LOAF

1 cup sugar
1/2 cup butter or margarine,
   softened
1 egg
1 2/3 cups flour
1 teaspoon baking powder

1/2 teaspoon salt
1/2 cup milk
1 1/2 teaspoons dried lemon peel
1/8 cup sugar
1/4 cup lemon juice

Preheat oven to 375 degrees. Using rotary beater, cream 1 cup sugar and butter in large bowl. Add egg and beat well. Sift together flour, baking powder and salt; stir into egg mixture. Add milk and lemon peel; combine well. Pour into well-greased 9x5-inch loaf pan. Bake 1 hour or until pick inserted in center comes out clean. Combine remaining sugar and lemon juice; pour over warm loaf while still in pan. Yields 1 loaf.

ORANGE BREAD

2 packages dry yeast
1 cup warm water
¼ cup butter or margarine,
    melted
½ cup sugar

1 egg, at room temperature
1 teaspoon salt
⅔ cup orange juice
5 to 5¼ cups flour
3 tablespoons orange rind

Dissolve yeast in water. Add butter, sugar, egg, salt and orange juice; combine thoroughly. Add 2 cups flour and orange rind; beat until smooth. Stir in about ½ of remaining flour. When dough becomes too stiff to stir, turn onto a lightly floured surface; knead in remaining flour. Place dough in a greased bowl; turn to grease all over. Cover and let rise 1 hour. Punch dough down; place in 2 well-greased 9x5-inch pans. Cover and let rise another hour. Preheat oven to 400 degrees. Bake 30 to 35 minutes. Yields 2 loaves.

BANANA PRUNE BREAD

2½ cups sifted flour
3 teaspoons baking powder
1 teaspoon salt
¼ teaspoon nutmeg
⅓ cup butter or margarine,
    softened
1 cup sugar

2 large eggs
1 cup mashed bananas (2 or 3)
1 tablespoon cooking liquid
    from prunes
1 cup cooked chopped prunes
½ cup chopped walnuts

Preheat oven to 350 degrees. Resift flour with baking powder, salt and nutmeg. Cream butter, sugar and eggs thoroughly. Add flour mixture, bananas and prune liquid alternately to creamed mixture. Blend. Fold in prunes and walnuts. Turn into one 9x5-inch or four 5½x3 ⅛-inch well-greased loaf pans. Place in lower third of oven. Bake 60 to 65 minutes for large loaf, 45 minutes for small ones or until pick inserted in center comes out clean. Remove and let stand 10 minutes before turning onto wire rack to cool. Yields 1 large or 4 small loaves.

THE COUNSELOR'S STRAWBERRY BREAD

3 cups flour
1 teaspoon soda
1 teaspoon salt
2 cups sugar
1 tablespoon cinnamon
20 ounces frozen strawberries,
    thawed

4 eggs, well beaten
1¼ cups cooking oil
1¼ cups chopped nuts
Red food coloring, if desired

Preheat oven to 350 degrees. Sift flour, soda, salt, sugar and cinnamon into large bowl. Stir in remaining ingredients; pour into two 9x5- or three 4x8-inch greased and floured loaf pans. Bake 1 hour or until pick inserted in center comes out clean. Cool thoroughly before removing from pan. Yields 2 or 3 loaves.

TIP: Use either sweetened or unsweetened strawberries—equally delicious!

BECKY'S BEST BREAKFAST BREAD

1½ cups corn flakes
2 cups flour
3 teaspoons baking powder
½ teaspoon salt
½ cup butter or margarine,
    softened

½ cup sugar
2 eggs
2 teaspoons orange peel
1 cup orange juice
½ cup raisins
½ cup finely chopped nuts

Preheat oven to 350 degrees. Crush corn flakes to ¾ cup. Stir in flour, baking powder and salt. Set aside. Beat butter and sugar in large bowl until light and fluffy. Add eggs and orange peel. Beat well. Stir in orange juice. Add dry ingredients, mixing only until combined. Stir in raisins and nuts. Spread in well-greased 9x5-inch loaf pan. Bake 50 minutes or until pick inserted near center comes out clean. Cool about 10 minutes before removing from pan. Cool completely before slicing. Yields 1 loaf.

APPLE CHEESE LOAF

4 cups sifted flour
3 teaspoons baking powder
1 teaspoon baking soda
2 teaspoons salt
1 cup butter or margarine,
   softened

1 1/3 cups sugar
4 eggs
2 large tart apples, pared, cored
   and shredded
1 cup (4 ounces) shredded
   sharp Cheddar cheese

Preheat oven to 350 degrees. Sift flour, baking powder, baking soda and salt together. Beat butter, sugar and eggs in a large bowl until fluffy. Stir in apples; add dry ingredients. Stir in cheese until thoroughly combined. Divide evenly into two well-greased 9x5-inch loaf pans. Bake 50 minutes or until center is firm. Cool 5 minutes in pan; then cool thoroughly on wire rack. Wrap loaves in foil or plastic wrap; store overnight to allow flavors to blend and to make slicing easier. Yields 2 loaves.

BLUEBERRY MUFFINS

1 to 1 1/2 cups blueberries (fresh,
   canned or frozen)
3 cups flour
1/2 cup granulated sugar
1 tablespoon baking powder
1 teaspoon salt

1/2 cup brown sugar
1/2 cup melted butter or
   margarine
3 large eggs
1 cup milk
Powdered sugar

Preheat oven to 400 degrees. Wash and dry blueberries. Sift flour, granulated sugar, baking powder and salt into a bowl. Add brown sugar and blend. Combine butter, eggs and milk. Stir into dry ingredients until just blended. Carefully fold in blueberries. Spoon into well-buttered muffin cups (either medium- or miniature-size) until 2/3 full. Bake 20 minutes or until browned. Dust with powdered sugar while muffins are hot. Yields 20 to 24 medium-size or 40 to 48 miniature-size muffins.

VARIATION: Substitute strawberries, raspberries, blackberries or loganberries for the blueberries. Hull if necessary and slice large berries in half.

COFFEE CAKE MUFFINS

1 cup flour
1/2 cup sugar
1 1/2 teaspoons baking powder
1/4 teaspoon salt
1/4 cup shortening or 1/3 cup
    butter or margarine

1 egg
1/2 cup milk
1 teaspoon vanilla extract

Preheat oven to 375 degrees. Sift flour, sugar, baking powder and salt together. Cut in the shortening or butter until flour mixture is crumbly. Beat egg with milk and vanilla. Add to flour mixture; stir until just blended. Divide batter equally among 12 greased muffin cups. Sprinkle with Topping (see recipe below); pat into batter gently. Bake 15 minutes or until muffins are golden brown and tops spring back when touched. Yields 12 muffins.

Topping:
1/3 cup brown sugar
1 1/2 teaspoons cinnamon
1/3 cup chopped walnuts

2 tablespoons butter or
    margarine, softened

Combine all ingredients in small bowl; mix well.

VARIATION: For an extra surprise, place a teaspoon of cherry preserves or thin slice of apple, peach or plum in the batter. Add Topping and bake as directed.

SOPAIPILLAS

4 cups flour
4 teaspoons baking powder
1 teaspoon salt
2 tablespoons shortening

1 1/2 cups water
Cooking oil
Cinnamon

Sift together flour, baking powder and salt. Cut in the shortening until mixture resembles coarse crumbs. Add enough of the water to make a soft dough that is easy to handle. Knead approximately 10 minutes. Let dough stand at least 30 minutes. Roll out on floured surface to 1/8-inch thickness. Cut into 3-inch squares. Deep fry in hot oil until golden on both sides. Sprinkle with cinnamon and serve immediately. Excellent with butter and honey. Serves 8 to 10.

COFFEE CAKE SUPREME

½ cup butter or margarine,
   softened
1 cup sugar
1 teaspoon soda
1 cup sour cream

2 eggs, at room temperature
1 teaspoon vanilla extract
1½ cups sifted flour
1½ teaspoons baking powder
Powdered sugar

Preheat oven to 350 degrees. In large bowl with rotary beater, cream butter. Add sugar and cream well. Combine soda and sour cream. In a separate bowl, beat eggs well. Add sour cream/soda mixture and vanilla to eggs. Sift flour and baking powder together. Add flour and sour cream/egg mixtures alternately to sugar and butter, beating well after each addition. Grease an 8- or 9-inch square baking pan or small bundt pan. Pour in half of batter; spread evenly. Sprinkle with half of the Topping (see recipe below). Pour remaining batter over Topping; spread evenly. Sprinkle evenly with remaining Topping; run fork over top to gently mix Topping with a little batter. Bake 30 to 35 minutes. Allow cake to remain in pan a few minutes after removing from oven. Turn onto rack to cool slightly. Just before serving, dust with powdered sugar. Yields 9 squares.

Topping:
½ cup brown sugar
1½ teaspoons cinnamon

¾ cup chopped pecans or
   walnuts

Combine all ingredients in small bowl; mix well.

BRIOCHE

1 package dry yeast	¹/₂ teaspoon salt
¹/₄ cup warm water	4 cups sifted flour
¹/₂ cup milk	3 eggs
³/₄ cup butter or margarine,	4 egg yolks
softened	Melted butter or margarine
¹/₄ cup sugar	1 tablespoon milk

Soften yeast in warm water; let stand 5 to 10 minutes. Scald milk. Combine butter, sugar and salt in large bowl; pour scalded milk over. Allow to stand until lukewarm. Stir in ¹/₂ cup flour, mixing thoroughly. Stir softened yeast; add to butter/flour mixture and combine thoroughly. Beat in 1¹/₂ cups flour. Add eggs and 3 egg yolks one at a time, beating well after each addition. Beat in enough of the remaining flour to form a soft dough. Beat thoroughly, at least 5 minutes. Turn into deep, buttered bowl just large enough to allow dough to double in size. Brush with melted butter. Cover with waxed paper and a towel; set aside in warm place to rise. When doubled in size, punch down with fist. Butter surface and cover again. Set in refrigerator 12 hours or overnight. Punch down occasionally as dough rises. When ready to bake, remove from refrigerator and place on lightly floured surface. Shape ²/₃ of dough into eighteen 2-inch balls. Place in buttered muffin cups or brioche pans. Form 18 small balls from remaining dough. Gently roll each smaller ball into a cone shape between palms of hands. Make an impression in center of each larger ball with finger; insert smaller balls, tip-down into impression. (These form the "top hats".) Cover loosely with a towel; set aside in warm place until doubled. Brush lightly with mixture of milk and remaining egg yolk. Preheat oven to 425 degrees. Bake 15 to 20 minutes or until golden brown. Yields 18.

NOTE: Although brioches require a lot of preparation time, they are really quite simple—and almost foolproof. Keep in the freezer to quickly "dress-up" simple scrambled eggs. Try the recipes in this book, (pages 18 and 29) but also experiment with other strong-flavored scrambled eggs. When ready to use, remove from freezer and thaw. Reheat on cookie sheet in 350 degree oven while preparing the eggs. Slice off the top, scoop out the center, fill with eggs and top with "hat".

Ever get tired of the same old ham, sausage or bacon question? There are many recipes throughout this cookbook that incorporate meat into the main dish—thus overcoming this dilemma. But don't forget about smoked pork chops, Italian sausage links or patties, dried beef and corned beef hash to add a little more variety to your menus. And these next recipes are sure to please and give your meals an extra lift!

BACON-A-DIFFERENT-WAY

Slices of bacon   Flour

Preheat broiler. Dredge bacon slices with flour, shaking off excess. Broil, turning once and watching carefully as it will burn easily.

HAM AND PINEAPPLE SLICES

1 cup cooked ground ham   2 tablespoons mayonnaise
1 teaspoon prepared mustard   4 slices pineapple, drained

Preheat oven to 400 degrees. Combine ham, mustard and mayonnaise by hand or in food processor. Spread on pineapple slices. Bake in ungreased 8-inch square baking dish 15 minutes or until heated through. Serves 2 to 4.

HAM PATTIES

14 to 16 ounces cooked ham,   Pepper to taste
   finely minced   Milk
2 eggs, beaten   Cooking Oil
1 cup cracker crumbs

Combine ham, eggs, cracker crumbs and pepper. If necessary, moisten with enough milk to shape into patties. Heat oil in large heavy skillet. Sauté patties until golden. Serves 4 to 6.

CORNED BEEF HASH PATTIES

1 (15-ounce) can corned beef
   hash
1 tablespoon prepared mustard
2 tablespoons chili sauce

2 tablespoons minced onion
Dash cayenne pepper
1 egg, beaten
Cooking oil

Combine corned beef hash, mustard, chili sauce, onion and pepper. Add egg; blend thoroughly. Shape mixture into 4 patties. Place in refrigerator at least 1 hour or until thoroughly chilled and easy to handle. In heavy skillet over low heat, brown both sides of patties in 2 to 3 tablespoons hot oil. Serves 4.

EMPANADAS

2 (3-ounce) packages cream
   cheese, softened
1 cup butter or margarine,
   softened

2 cups flour

Two days before serving, cream all ingredients with an electric mixer until dough is smooth. Refrigerate overnight. The day before serving, roll out dough on a lightly floured surface to ¼-inch thickness. Cut into desired size and shape. Place equal amounts of Filling (see recipe below) near center of each. Fold in half and seal edges with tines of a fork. Place on ungreased cookie sheet; cover well with plastic wrap and again refrigerate overnight. On the day of serving, preheat oven to 400 degrees. Bake 10 to 12 minutes. Serve hot. Yields 20 to 24 empanadas.

Filling:
2 (2¼-ounce) cans deviled
   ham

⅔ cup shredded Monterey Jack
   or muenster cheese

Combine ingredients and mix well.

TIP: Cut the dough into 2- or 3-inch circles or squares that can be folded into small squares, triangles or half circles. Serve the smaller ones as an hor d'oeuvre at your next Mexican-theme brunch and the larger ones as a side dish to round out a South of the Border menu.

CRAB VERMICELLI

8 ounces vermicelli, cooked
   according to package
   directions
1 pound fresh or canned
   crabmeat, drained and
   flaked

2 cups (8 ounces) shredded
   sharp Cheddar cheese

Preheat oven to 350 degrees. Layer vermicelli, crabmeat, Sauce (see recipe below) and cheese in greased 2½-quart casserole. Bake 30 minutes. Serves 8.

Sauce:
10 ounces bottled ketchup
3 teaspoons Worcestershire
   sauce

1 cup butter or margarine
½ teaspoon dry mustard

Combine all ingredients. Simmer until butter is melted and flavors are blended.

SAUSAGE AND FRUIT CRÊPES

¾ pound bulk sausage,
   cooked and crumbled
3 cooking apples, cored
   and peeled
¼ cup raisins
1 teaspoon cinnamon

1 tablespoon butter or
   margarine
8 crêpes, warmed (see recipes
   page 31)
Brown sugar
Toasted almonds

Drain sausage on paper towels and keep warm. Cut apples into thin slices. In a medium skillet, simmer apples, raisins and cinnamon in butter until apples are tender, about 10 minutes. Stir in sausage; combine well. Spoon into crêpes and roll. Top with sprinkle of brown sugar and toasted almonds. Serves 8.

ORANGE-STRAWBERRY PRESERVES

3¼ cups sugar
1 (10-ounce) carton frozen
   strawberries, thawed
1 (6-ounce) can frozen orange
   juice, thawed

2 tablespoons lime or lemon
   juice
Red food coloring (optional)

Combine sugar and strawberries in a large saucepan; mix well. Over high heat, bring to full rolling boil. Boil 1 minute, stirring constantly. Remove from heat; stir in orange juice concentrate and lime or lemon juice. Skim off foam with metal spoon. Return to heat; bring to boil and boil 1 minute, stirring constantly. Again, skim off foam. Add food coloring. Pour into warmed jelly glasses and seal with hot paraffin. Yields approximately 4 cups.

JALAPEÑO JELLY

¾ cup chopped green pepper,
   with membrane removed
⅓ cup sliced fresh jalapeño
   peppers, seeded
1 cup water
1 cup apple cider vinegar

4-5 drops green food coloring
   (optional)
5 cups sugar
2 (3-ounce) pouches liquid
   pectin

Combine peppers, water, vinegar, food coloring and sugar in large kettle; bring to rapid boil, stirring constantly. Boil hard 1 minutes. Add pectin. Return to rapid boil; boil hard 1 minute, stirring constantly. Remove from heat. Continue stirring 2-3 minutes. Let cool 10 minutes, stirring occasionally. Ladle into 6 half-pint jars that are clean and hot, distributing peppers evenly. Seal jars and process 5 minutes in boiling water bath. Remove from bath and cool. Invert jars after 1 hour to distribute peppers; shake every half hour as necessary (will take 3 to 6 hours to set). Yields 3 pints.

Contributed by NEW CANAAN COMPANY.

VARIATION: To make HOT JALAPEÑO JELLY, use ¼ cup chopped red bell peppers instead of the green and 1 cup *unseeded* sliced jalapeño peppers. Substitute ¼ cup jalapeño sauce (purchased) for the apple cider vinegar.

TRY THIS: Drizzle HOT JALAPEÑO JELLY over cream cheese. Serve with crackers as a quick appetizer for a Mexican-theme brunch.

APRICOT MARMALADE

1 pound dried apricots
2 cups water
1 (20½-ounce) can crushed
   pineapple

Grated rind of 1 orange
1 cup orange juice
4 cups sugar

Combine apricots and water in large saucepan; cook uncovered 20 minutes. Add remaining ingredients; cook over low heat 45 minutes stirring occasionally to prevent scorching. Pour into sterilized jars and seal with paraffin. Yields 3 pints.

POPPY SEED DRESSING

1½ cups sugar
2 teaspoons dry mustard
2 teaspoons salt
⅔ cup vinegar

3 tablespoons onion juice
2 cups salad oil
3 tablespoons poppy seeds

In a blender, mix sugar, mustard, salt and vinegar. Add onion juice; blend on medium speed until thoroughly combined. With blender running, add oil in a slow steady stream; continue to blend until mixture thickens. Add poppy seeds and beat a few seconds. Store in a covered jar in refrigerator. Shake well before serving over your favorite fruits. Yields approximately 4 cups.

NOTE: Dressing lasts for several months if it does not get too cold or hot.

AVOCADO DRESSING

2 medium avocados, peeled
   and seeded
½ (4-ounce) can chopped green
   chilies, drained
4 tablespoons lime or lemon
   juice

3 green onions, finely sliced
2 cloves garlic, finely minced
1 teaspoon salt

Mash avocados with a fork; add chilies, juice, onions, garlic and salt. Blend thoroughly. Place in a tightly covered container and chill until served. Yields approximately 1 cup.

HINT: A green salad adorned with Avocado Dressing becomes a fitting accompaniment for a Mexican brunch!

BECKY'S BLENDER HOLLANDAISE

4 egg yolks
Pinch salt

3 tablespoons lemon juice
1 cup butter, melted

Place egg yolks, salt and lemon juice in a blender. Whip 1 minute. Turn blender to low speed and slowly add hot butter in a steady stream. Continue to blend until thickened. Serve at once. Yields approximately 1½ cups.

There are many recipes for these two staples of Mexican menus—most of which are much more complex. These are both very simple—and the best! Use both where called for in this cookbook, or serve with chips and crudites for a quick and delicious appetizer.

GAYLE'S GLORIOUS GUACAMOLE

2 ripe avocados, peeled and
    seeded
2 tablespoons lemon juice

1 teaspoon salt
1 tablespoon grated onion

Mash avocados thoroughly with fork. Add remaining ingredients and combine. Chill until time to serve. Yields approximately 1¼ cups.

TIP: If recipe is increased, add salt to taste.

SALSA

1 (28-ounce) can whole
    tomatoes
1 large onion

Salt to taste
Pickled jalapeño peppers to
    taste (about 3)

Combine all ingredients in blender. Whirl until smooth. Taste for seasonings. Cover and store in refrigerator. Yields approximately 2 cups.

NOTE: Salsa lasts in the refrigerator several weeks.

MEXICAN HOT CHOCOLATE

6 cups milk
3 squares unsweetened
   chocolate

3 tablespoons sugar
1½ teaspoons ground cinnamon
Cinnamon sticks

Heat milk in large saucepan just until bubbles appear around edge. Stir in chocolate, sugar and cinnamon. Continue heating until chocolate melts. Beat with rotary beater until smooth. Return to heat and bring to serving temperature. Beat again with rotary beater until frothy. Pour into heated mugs and garnish with a cinnamon stick if desired. Serves 6.

HOT CRANBERRY TEA

1 (12-ounce) package fresh
   cranberries, rinsed
2½ quarts water
2 cups sugar
3 sticks cinnamon

1 (6-ounce) can frozen orange
   juice, thawed
2 orange juice cans water
½ cup lemon juice

Cook cranberries in 2 quarts water until tender. Strain off juice; discard hulls and pulp. Add 2 cups water, sugar and cinnamon to cranberry juice in saucepan; simmer 10 minutes. Cool. Add orange juice concentrate, water and lemon juice. Heat through and serve. Serves 10 to 12.

HOT CRANBERRY CIDER

1½ quarts cranberry juice
1 (12-ounce) can frozen
   orange juice, thawed

1½ orange juice cans water
Cinnamon to taste

Combine cranberry juice, orange juice concentrate and water in large saucepan. Heat to boiling; boil a few minutes to blend flavors. Add cinnamon. Serves 8 to 10.

SPICED TEA

2½ cups sugar
2 cups instant orange-flavored
   breakfast drink mix
1 cup instant tea granules

⅓ cup lemonade drink mix
1 tablespoon cinnamon
1 teaspoon cloves

Combine all ingredients; stir to mix well. Store in air-tight container. Yields approximately 6 cups.

TO SERVE: Place 3 heaping teaspoons (or to taste) in a cup and fill with boiling water. Stir and serve immediately.

BRUNCH COCKTAIL

¾ cup orange juice, chilled
¼ cup cranberry juice, chilled
¼ cup vodka

1 tablespoon lime juice, chilled
Garnish

Combine all ingredients and pour over ice in tall glass. Garnish with strawberry and orange slice. Serves 1.

KIR

1 tablespoon crème de cassis   2½ cups chilled dry white wine

Combine ingredients and pour into chilled wine glasses or over ice. Serve immediately. Serves 6.

GEORGIA'S FRENCH "75"

1 ounce brandy
1 ounce Triple Sec

Orange juice
Champagne

Pour brandy and Triple Sec over ice in 8-ounce glass. Add orange juice to approximately ½-inch from top of glass. Fill with champagne and stir. Serves 1.

WHEN
IT'S TIME TO
ENTERTAIN

The Morning After
The Night Before
New Year's Day Brunch

Hors D'oeuvre
Salsa

Chips   Crudites

Entrée
Dried Beef and Eggs
Served in
Giant Popovers

Vegetable
Hot Spinach Salad   Cheese Garlic Grits

Fruit
Wide Awake Fruit Salad

Beverage
Coffee   Hot Cranberry Tea
Bloody Maries

DRIED BEEF AND EGGS

16 eggs, lightly beaten
1/4 teaspoon salt
1 cup evaporated milk

4 tablespoons butter or
    margarine

Preheat oven to 275 degrees. Combine eggs with salt and milk. In a large skillet, scramble egg mixture in butter. Place a small amount of the Beefy Sauce (see recipe below) in a greased 3-quart casserole; top with a layer of eggs. Repeat layers, ending with sauce. Cover and bake 1 hour. Serves 8 to 10.

Beefy Sauce:
4 slices bacon, diced
4 (2 1/2-ounce) jars dried beef,
    torn into bite-size pieces
2 (4-ounce) cans sliced
    mushrooms, drained

4 tablespoons butter or
    margarine
1/2 cup flour
4 cups milk
Pepper to taste

In a large skillet, fry bacon until almost crisp. Add beef, mushrooms, and butter to the bacon; heat through. Add flour, milk and pepper; cook until sauce is slightly thickened.

HINT: When assembled, this tempting dish may be refrigerated and baked when needed. Increase the oven temperature to 300 degrees and the time to 1 1/2 hours.

GIANT POPOVERS

Butter
Oil
4 large eggs
2 cups milk

2 tablespoons cooking oil
2 cups flour
1/2 teaspoon salt

Preheat oven to 400 degrees. Generously grease two 9x9-inch glass baking dishes with butter and oil. Set in oven to heat 3 to 5 minutes. Beat eggs with wire whisk until light. Add milk and oil; whisk until thoroughly blended. Add flour and salt; whisk until smooth. Pour batter equally into hot baking dishes. Bake 30 minutes; lower temperature to 350 degrees and bake 10 more minutes or until cavity is completely baked. Yields 2 popovers.

NOTE: Each Giant Popover is an open shell with sides about 3 inches high—ready to fill with scrambled eggs. To serve, cut into wedges and place on serving plates using a wide spatula. Beautiful!

South Of The Border Brunch

Hors D'oeuvre
Empanadas

Entrée
Sunrise Nachos

Condiments
Gayle's Glorious Guacamole   Salsa
Green Onions   Ripe Olives
Sour Cream

Bread
Flour Tortillas   Assorted Preserves
Honey Butter

Fruit
Salad Mexicana

Beverage
Margaritas   Coffee

SUNRISE NACHOS

1 pound bulk sausage,
    crumbled
1 small onion, chopped
1 (4-ounce) can diced green
    chilies
Corn-flavored tortilla chips
    (about 4 cups)
2 cups (8 ounces) shredded
    Cheddar or Monterey Jack
    cheese

4 to 8 eggs
Gayle's Glorious Guacamole
    (see page 102)
Sour cream
Sliced green onions
Sliced pitted ripe olives
Salsa (bottled or see page 102)

Preheat broiler. In a medium skillet, sauté sausage and onion over medium-high heat, stirring until lightly browned. Drain off fat and stir in chilies. Set aside. Divide chips between 4 greased individual ramekins or oven-proof bowls. Top each dish of chips with an equal amount of sausage mixture. Sprinkle each with about ¼ cup shredded cheese and keep warm. Poach, fry until softly set, or scramble eggs. Place eggs on the sausage mixture; sprinkle each with some of the remaining cheese. Broil just long enough to melt cheese. To serve, pass Guacamole, sour cream, green onions, ripe olives and Salsa. Spoon over each serving according to taste. Serves 4.

Summer Special Brunch

Entrée
Baked Mushroom Delight

Vegetable
Karen's Zucchini Florentine

Fruit
Summer Special Salad

Bread
Lemon Loaf   Orange Bread

Beverage
Spiced Tea   Screw Drivers

Assorted Juices

BAKED MUSHROOM DELIGHT

½ pound fresh mushrooms,
  sliced
2 tablespoons butter or
  margarine
8 strips bacon, fried crisp,
  drained and crumbled

3 cups (12 ounces) shredded
  Monterey Jack cheese
8 eggs, beaten
¼ teaspoon salt
Pepper to taste

Preheat oven to 275 degrees. Sauté mushrooms in butter; place on bottom of a well-greased 8-inch square baking dish. Top with bacon and then the cheese. Combine eggs, salt and pepper; pour over layered ingredients. Bake 45 minutes to 1 hour or until center is set and top is golden. Serves 4 to 6.

TO PREPARE IN ADVANCE: Assemble up to the point of pouring the egg mixture over the layered ingredients. This "Delight" can also be frozen after baking and reheated.

KAREN'S ZUCCHINI FLORENTINE

2 medium zucchini
1 tablespoon minced onion
6 tablespoons butter or
  margarine
1 (10-ounce) package frozen
  chopped spinach, cooked
  and squeezed dry

Salt and pepper to taste
Pinch of garlic powder
¼ teaspoon nutmeg
¼ cup grated Parmesan cheese

Preheat oven to 350 degrees. Wash zucchini; trim ends and split lengthwise. Scoop out seeds with melon baller, leaving an indentation for the stuffing. Blanch the zucchini by dropping into 4 quarts boiling water for 5 minutes. Remove and immediately place in cold water. Remove and pat dry. Sauté onions in 4 tablespoons butter until onions are limp, about 5 minutes. Add spinach, salt, pepper, garlic powder and nutmeg. Stuff the zucchini with equal amounts of spinach mixture. Place in greased baking dish; sprinkle with Parmesan cheese. Dot with remaining 2 tablespoons butter. Bake 10 minutes or until heated through. Serves 4.

Before the Game Brunch

Hors D'oeuvre
Mexican Muffins

Entrée
Cheesy Mexican Puff

Vegetable
Mexican Potato Cakes

Fruit
Overnight Fruit Compote

Dessert
Sopaipillas
Powdered Sugar   Cinnamon
Honey Butter

Beverage
Mexican Hot Chocolate   Coffee
Tequila Sunrise

CHEESY MEXICAN PUFF

3½ cups (14 ounces) shredded
    Monterey Jack cheese
3½ cups (14 ounces) shredded
    sharp Cheddar cheese
1 (7-ounce) can diced green
    chilies
2 tomatoes, peeled, seeded and
    chopped
1 (2¼-ounce) can sliced black
    olives, drained

½ cup flour
6 eggs, separated
1 (5¼-ounce) can evaporated
    milk
½ teaspoon salt
½ teaspoon oregano leaves
¼ teaspoon ground cumin
¼ teaspoon pepper
¼ teaspoon cream of tartar

Preheat oven to 300 degrees. Stir together the cheeses, chilies, tomatoes, olives and 2 tablespoons of the flour until blended. Spread mixture evenly in well-greased shallow 3-quart baking dish. In a small bowl, beat the egg yolks. Alternately add remaining flour and milk, beating until smooth. Stir in salt, oregano, cumin and pepper. In a large bowl, beat the egg whites with cream of tartar until stiff but able to form moist peaks. Fold egg yolk mixture into the whites. Spoon over cheese mixture in casserole. Bake 1 hour or until top is golden brown and firm to touch. Let stand about 15 minutes before serving. Serves 10 to 12.

MEXICAN POTATO CAKES

2 cups mashed potatoes (do
    not use instant)
¼ cup shredded Cheddar cheese
1 egg, lightly beaten
1 egg yolk, lightly beaten

¼ cup dry bread crumbs
1 teaspoon minced onion
½ teaspoon salt
¼ teaspoon chili powder
Cooking oil

Combine potatoes, cheese, egg, egg yolk, bread crumbs, onion, salt and chili powder. Mix until well blended. Pour oil ¼-inch deep into heavy skillet. When moderately hot, drop potato mixture by rounded teaspoons into oil; flatten slightly with a spatula. When golden brown on the underside (about 3 to 5 minutes) turn and cook until golden brown on the other side. Serves 4.

Meet You At The Bottom of the Hill Skier's Brunch

Entrée
Jeannie's Sausage Soufflé

Vegetable
Texas Hash   Barbara's Broccoli Bake

Fruit
Hot Fruit Salad

Bread
Apple Cheese Bread   Banana Prune Bread

Beverage
Coffee   Hot Cranberry Cider

JEANNIE'S SAUSAGE SOUFFLÉ

6 slices bread, crust removed
Butter or margarine
1 pound bulk sausage,
    crumbled, cooked and
    drained
4 cups (16 ounces) shredded
    sharp Cheddar cheese

2 cups light cream
1 teaspoon salt
1 teaspoon dry mustard
6 eggs, well beaten

Spread both sides of bread with butter. Place in well-greased 9x13-inch glass baking dish. Cover bread with the sausage; sprinkle cheese over all. Mix a small portion of cream with salt and mustard until it is well combined. Add remaining cream and eggs. Blend. Pour over layers in baking dish. Cover and refrigerate overnight. When ready to serve, preheat oven to 350 degrees. Bake uncovered 40 to 45 minutes. Serves 8 to 10.

VARIATION: Substitute 1 pound bacon, fried crisp and crumbled, for the sausage.

HOT FRUIT SALAD

1 (12-ounce) package dried
    pitted prunes
1 (6-ounce) package dried
    apricots
1 (13½-ounce) can pineapple
    chunks, undrained

1 (21-ounce) can cherry pie
    filling
1¾ cups water
¼ cup dry white wine

Preheat oven to 350 degrees. Arrange prunes, apricots and pineapple in buttered 9-inch square glass baking dish. Combine pie filling, water and wine; pour over fruit. Cover and bake 1½ hours. Serve warm. Serves 8.

OR TRY THIS: Place all ingredients in a crockpot. Cover and cook on Low 7 to 8 hours or on High 3 to 4 hours.

Santa Claus's Favorite Brunch

Hors D'oeuvre
Cheddar Olive Spread
on
English Muffins

Entrée
A Quartet of Delectable Quiches
Swiss
Spinach
Mushroom
Sherried-Crab

Vegetable
Baked Savory Tomatoes

Fruit
Brandied Fruit Compote

Beverage
Coffee   Assorted Juices
Brunch Cocktail

SWISS QUICHE

2 cups heavy cream
4 eggs
¾ teaspoon salt
1 cup (4 ounces) shredded
    Swiss cheese

1 (9-inch) deep dish pastry shell
1 tablespoon butter or
    margarine, softened

Preheat oven to 425 degrees. Mix cream, eggs and salt with wire whisk or fork until well blended. Stir in cheese. Spread pastry shell with butter. Pour cream mixture into pastry shell. Bake 15 minutes. Turn temperature down to 325 degrees; bake 35 minutes longer or until knife inserted in center comes out clean. Serves 6.

SPINACH QUICHE

2 tablespoons minced green
    onions
3 tablespoons butter or
    margarine
2 cups heavy cream
4 eggs
¾ teaspoon salt

1 (10-ounce) package frozen
    chopped spinach, thawed
    and well drained
⅛ teaspoon nutmeg
⅛ teaspoon pepper
1 (9-inch) deep dish
    pastry shell

Preheat oven to 425 degrees. In a small skillet over medium heat, sauté green onions in 2 tablespoons butter until tender, about 5 minutes. Mix cream, eggs and salt with wire whisk or fork until well blended. Stir in green onion mixture, spinach, nutmeg and pepper. Spread pastry shell with remaining tablespoon butter. Pour cream mixture into pastry shell. Bake 15 minutes. Turn temperature down to 325 degrees; bake 35 minutes longer or until knife inserted in center comes out clean. Serves 6.

MUSHROOM QUICHE

½ pound fresh mushrooms,
   thinly sliced
2 tablespoons minced green
   onions
5 tablespoons butter or
   margarine

⅛ teaspoon pepper
2 cups heavy cream
4 eggs
1 teaspoon salt
1 (9-inch) deep dish pastry shell

Preheat oven to 425 degrees. In a medium skillet over medium-high heat, sauté mushrooms and green onion in 4 tablespoons butter until tender, about 5 minutes. Stir frequently. Sprinkle pepper over all. Mix cream, eggs and salt with wire whisk or fork until well blended. Stir in mushroom mixture. Spread pastry shell with remaining tablespoon butter. Pour cream mixture into pastry shell. Bake 15 minutes. Turn temperature down to 325 degrees; bake 35 minutes longer or until knife inserted in center comes out clean. Serves 6.

SHERRIED-CRAB QUICHE

2 tablespoons minced green
   onions
4 tablespoons butter or
   margarine
2 cups heavy cream
4 eggs
¾ teaspoon salt

2 (6-ounce) packages frozen
   snow crab, thawed and
   drained well
2 tablespoons dry sherry
⅛ teaspoon cayenne pepper
1 (9-inch) deep dish pastry shell

Preheat oven to 425 degrees. In a small skillet over medium heat, sauté green onions in 3 tablespoons butter until tender, about 5 minutes. Mix cream, eggs and salt with wire whisk or fork until well blended. Stir in green onion mixture, crab, sherry and cayenne pepper. Spread pastry shell with remaining tablespoon butter. Pour cream mixture into pastry shell. Bake 15 minutes. Turn temperature down to 325 degrees; bake 35 minutes longer or until knife inserted in center comes out clean. Serves 6.

Try one or all of this quartet of quiches made from the same basic recipe—the flavors are marvelously compatible in any combination! And they can all be reheated after baking—simply cover with foil and bake in 325 degree oven 40 minutes or until heated through.

BRANDIED FRUIT COMPOTE

2 (10-ounce) packages pitted
   dried prunes
Walnut halves
1 (29-ounce) can fruits for
   salad, drained
1 (11-ounce) can mandarin
   orange slices, drained

1 (20-ounce) can pineapple
   chunks, drained
1 (21-ounce) can cherry pie
   filling
1 (11-ounce) package dried
   apricots
¾ cup apricot brandy

Preheat oven to 350 degrees. Stuff prunes with walnuts. Combine remaining fruits; add stuffed prunes. Pour brandy over all and gently toss to combine. Bake in greased 9x13-inch glass baking dish 30 minutes. Serve hot or cold. Serves 16.

NOTES

INDEX

BECKY'S BRUNCH & BREAKFAST BOOK
P.O. Box 5892
Austin, Texas 78763

Please send me _____ copies of **BECKY'S BRUNCH &
BREAKFAST BOOK** at $7.95 per copy plus $1.50 for postage and
handling. Texas residents add 5⅛% (.41/copy) sales tax. Please
gift wrap _____ copies at $1.00/copy.

Enclosed is my check or money order for _____ made payable
to **BECKY'S BRUNCH & BREAKFAST BOOK.**

NAME _____

ADDRESS_____

CITY _____ STATE _____ ZIP _____

SEND GIFT-WRAPPED COPY TO THE FOLLOWING ADDRESS:

NAME _____

ADDRESS_____

CITY _____ STATE _____ ZIP _____

Attach information for additional gift-wrapped copies. An attractive
gift card with your name will be enclosed with each gift cookbook.

BECKY'S BRUNCH & BREAKFAST BOOK
P.O. Box 5892
Austin, Texas 78763

Please send me _____ copies of **BECKY'S BRUNCH &
BREAKFAST BOOK** at $7.95 per copy plus $1.50 for postage and
handling. Texas residents add 5⅛% (.41/copy) sales tax. Please
gift wrap _____ copies at $1.00/copy.

Enclosed is my check or money order for _____ made payable
to **BECKY'S BRUNCH & BREAKFAST BOOK.**

NAME _____

ADDRESS_____

CITY _____ STATE _____ ZIP _____

SEND GIFT-WRAPPED COPY TO THE FOLLOWING ADDRESS:

NAME _____

ADDRESS_____

CITY _____ STATE _____ ZIP _____

Attach information for additional gift-wrapped copies. An attractive
gift card with your name will be enclosed with each gift cookbook.

Reorder Additional Copies

Possessing three degrees from various Texas institutions (none of which are in Home Economics), Rebecca Walker has pursued such diverse professional fields as social work, dental hygiene and real estate. Throughout, one thing has remained constant: her love of cooking and joy in preparing and eating breakfast, both leisurely and "on the run". An adventuresome cook, she made it her business to develop, revise, test and collect breakfast and brunch recipes, a task all the more difficult as few cookbooks were available. Her interest in organizing her recipes for personal use led to the development of **Becky's Brunch & Breakfast Book.**

A resident of Austin, Texas, Ms. Walker is currently working on a new cookbook.